Wonderlic SLE Test Study Guide with Scholastic Level Exam Practice Tests

Wonderlic and Wonderlic Scholastic Level Exam are registered trademarks of Wonderlic, Inc, which is not affiliated with and does not endorse these materials.

Wonderlic SLE Test Study Guide with Scholastic Level Exam Practice Tests

© COPYRIGHT 2017, 2020. Exam SAM Study Aids & Media dba www.examsam.com

All rights reserved. No part of this publication may be reproduced, stored in a retrieval system, or transmitted, in any form or by any means, electronic, mechanical, photocopying, recording, or otherwise, without the prior written permission of the copyright owner.

ISBN 13: 978-1-949282-55-9

NOTE: Wonderlic and Wonderlic Scholastic Level Exam are registered trademarks of Wonderlic, Inc., which is not affiliated with and does not endorse these materials.

TABLE OF CONTENTS

Wonderlic SLE Format and Question Types	1
Math Word Problems	1
Logic and Reasoning Problems	1
Verbal Analysis Questions	2
General Knowledge Questions	2
Wonderlic SLE Quick Test	2
Watching the Time on the Wonderlic SLE	3
Wonderlic SLE Scores	4
Wonderlic SLE Practice Test 1:	
Adding Whole Numbers	5
Logic and Reasoning	5
Monetary Units	5
Identifying Duplicates in Numerical Lists	6
Comparing Numbers to Identify the Largest Value	6
Understanding Proverbs and Similar Expressions	6
Length and Linear Measurements	7
Understanding the Relationship Between Two Words	7
Working with Percentages	7
Analogies of Use and Function	8
Comparing Numbers to Find the Middle Value	8
Rearranging Words to Form a Sentence	8
Greatest Multiple of a Number	8
Identifying the Word That is Different from the Group – Nouns	9

Ordering Numbers from Greatest to Least	9
Finding the Missing Word in a Proverb	9
Math Word Problems with Multiple Operations	10
Numerical Series and Sequences	10
Analogies of Place	11
Smallest Multiple of a Number	11
Identifying Synonyms	11
Rate, Time, and Distance	12
Visual Data Representations	12
Finding the Missing Value in the Calculation of an Average	13
Working with Fractional Values	14
Forming Words from Anagrams	14
Ordering Numbers from Least to Greatest	14
Understanding Antonyms	15
Calculating Fractional Parts of a Whole	15
Identifying Duplicates in Lists of Letters with Punctuation	16
Calculating Discounted Prices	16
Identifying the Word That is Different from the Group – Adjectives	17
Analysis of Geometric Figures in a Series	17
Distance Traveled and Miles per Hour	18
Ratios and Proportions	18
Quick Identification of Months and Dates	19
Finding the Product of Two Numbers	19
Calculating Percentage Discounts	20

Analogies of Cause and Effect	20
Profit and Mark-Up of Cost	20
Following Instructions to Form a 3-D Figure	21
Wonderlic SLE Practice Test 2	23
Wonderlic SLE Practice Test 3	36
Wonderlic SLE Practice Test 4	51
Answer Key	65
Answers and Explanations:	
Wonderlic SLE Practice Test 1	73
Wonderlic SLE Practice Test 2	83
Wonderlic SLE Practice Test 3	92
Wonderlic SLE Practice Test 4	101
Appendix 1 – 40 Math Warm-Up Exercises	108
Appendix 2 – Solutions to the Math Warm-Up Exercises	113

WONDERLIC SLE FORMAT AND QUESTION TYPES

The Wonderlic Scholastic Level Exam, also known as the Wonderlic SLE, contains fifty questions that you will need to answer in 12 minutes.

Some questions will be multiple choice, with answer options provided. Other questions will be open response, for which you will need to work out the answer on your own.

The questions on the Wonderlic SLE can be placed into four broad categories: math word problems, logic and reasoning problems, verbal analysis questions on the English language, and general knowledge questions.

You will see different types of questions in each of these four categories:

Math Word Problems

- Whole numbers
- Money and profit problems
- Fractions and mixed numbers
- Decimals and percentages
- Rates, ratios, and proportions
- Calculating averages
- Lengths and linear values
- Evaluation of visual data

Logic and Reasoning Problems

- Geometric figure analysis
- Recognizing patterns
- Following instructions to form 3-D figures
- Using reasoning to determine the validity of statements

Verbal Analysis Questions

- Analogies
- Rearranging words to form sentences
- Comparing words in pairs and groups
- Synonyms and antonyms
- Advanced English vocabulary
- Sentence completion
- English proverbs and expressions
- Anagrams – rearranging letters to form words

General Knowledge Questions

- Recognizing dates
- Comparing and ordering values
- Identifying duplications in lists
- Recognizing the smallest or largest number

You will see all of the above types of questions in this study guide. Be sure to read the explanations for each question at the back of this publication to gain more strategies on how to answer each type of question on the exam.

The questions will be delivered in a random order on the real exam, so the questions will not be grouped into the discrete categories indicated above. Likewise, the questions in the practice tests in this study guide are not placed into groups.

Quick Test: Note that a short version of the Wonderlic SLE, known as the Quick Test, is also available. If you are offered the Quick Test, you will need to answer 30 questions in 8 minutes.

WATCHING THE TIME ON THE WONDERLIC SCHOLASTIC LEVEL EXAM

Read the following tips to gain strategies on how to answer questions efficiently on the Wonderlic exam:

- **Calculators** – Note that calculators are not allowed on the Wonderlic test.

- **Pace yourself while practicing** – Since most students fail even to answer all of the questions on the real exam, time yourself as you attempt the practice tests in this study guide. Try to answer all fifty questions in each practice test within twelve minutes.

- **Answering math and logic problems** – You should be able to answer basic arithmetic and verbal questions in under 7 seconds each. This leaves more time for the math and logic questions.

- **Preview the question** – Read the question before you read any information related to the question. This helps you anticipate what to look for.

- **Use scratch paper only when necessary** – Do math on-screen mentally if you can. You will lose valuable time writing on your scratch paper if you don't need to use it.

- **Do math mentally** – Sometimes you may not even need to calculate. Just estimate the result in your head and see which answer choice is the closest.

WONDERLIC SCHOLASTIC LEVEL EXAM SCORES

- **Know what score you need to achieve** – The score you need to get on the Wonderlic SLE varies, depending on which college you plan on attending.
    - 25 out of 50 is usually considered average, although top students may be able to score 45 out of 50.
    - To know the exact score that you need, you should inquire at your college's testing and placement office.
- **Tally your score as you practice** – You may wish to calculate your score manually as you check your answers to each practice test. This will help you chart your progress as you move through the material in the study guide.

WONDERLIC SLE PRACTICE TEST 1

Instructions: To simulate exam conditions, you should finish all 50 questions in each practice test in 12 minutes. You may wish to complete the math warm-up exercises in Appendix 1 before starting the practice tests.

Adding Whole Numbers

1) What is 1,594 + 23,786?
   A) 24,380
   B) 25,380
   C) 24,270
   D) 25,270

Logic and Reasoning

2) Assume the first two statements are true. Is the third one also true?
   The woman is playing golf.
   Everyone playing golf wears a blue shirt.
   The woman is wearing a blue shirt.
   A) True
   B) False
   C) Not certain

Monetary Units

3) A club has 25 members. If each member pays $15 in annual fees, how much money will the club collect in total for the membership fees?
   A) $375
   B) $355
   C) $325
   D) $290

Identifying Duplicates in Numerical Lists

4) How many of the pairs below are duplicates?

1896775	1896755
36718231	36718231
10010023	10010123
5618253	5618253
4610402	4610402

Comparing Numbers to Identify the Largest Value

5) Which of the following is the greatest?
   A) 0.350
   B) 0.035
   C) 0.053
   D) 0.3035

Understanding Proverbs and Similar Expressions

6) Which proverb is most similar to the one below?

   That's a cock and bull story.

   A) You're just clutching at straws.
   B) That doesn't hold water.
   C) Every cloud has a silver lining.
   D) The chicken is coming home to roost.

Length and Linear Measurements

7) A farmer is going to buy fence panels to put up a fence along one side of his field. Each panel is 8 feet 6 inches long. He needs 11 panels to cover the entire side of the field. How long is the field?
   A) 60 feet 6 inches
   B) 72 feet 8 inches
   C) 93 feet 6 inches
   D) 102 feet 8 inches

Understanding the Relationship Between Two Words

8) Which phrase below best describes the relationship between these two words:

   CONCEAL   OBSCURE

   A) They have similar meanings.
   B) They have contradictory meanings.
   C) They have unrelated meanings.

Working with Percentages

9) In a class which has x students, $s\%$ of the students have been absent this semester. Which of the following represents the number of students who have not been absent this semester?
   A) $100(s - x)$
   B) $(100\% - s\%) \times x$
   C) $(100\% - s\%) \div x$
   D) $(1 - s)x$

Analogies of Use and Function

10) Drive is to car as:
   A) Plow is to tractor
   B) House is to building
   C) Eat is to restaurant
   D) Cook is to oven

Comparing Numbers to Find the Middle Value

11) Which one of the following values is between 0.0007 and 0.0021?
   A) 0.0012
   B) 0.0006
   C) 0.0022
   D) 0.022

Rearranging Words to Form a Sentence

12) Rearrange the following words to form a sentence:

   rolling moss gathers no stone a

Greatest Multiple of a Number

13) A charity has to pay $3,700 up-front for costs and then pays $500 per project it undertakes. If the charity has $40,000 at the start, what is the greatest number of projects that can be completed?
   A) 72
   B) 73
   C) 74
   D) 79

Identifying the Word That is Different from the Group – Nouns

14) Which word below is most different to the others?

    Tractor

    Cow

    Farmer

    Horse

    Hay

Ordering Numbers from Greatest to Least

15) Which of the following shows the numbers ordered from greatest to least?
   A) $-1/3$, $1/7$, 1, $1/5$
   B) $-1/3$, $1/7$, $1/5$, 1
   C) $-1/3$, 1, $1/7$, $1/5$
   D) 1, $1/5$, $1/7$, $-1/3$

Finding the Missing Word in a Proverb

16) You can't make a(n) _____ without breaking a few eggs.
   A) cake
   B) recipe
   C) omelet
   D) feast

Math Word Problems with Multiple Operations

17) During each flight, a flight attendant must count the number of passengers on board the aircraft. The morning flight had 52 passengers more than the evening flight, and there were 540 passengers in total on the two flights that day. How many passengers were there on the evening flight?

   A) 244
   B) 296
   C) 488
   D) 540

Logic and Deductive Reasoning – Advanced Questions

18) Assume the first two statements are true. Is the third one also true?
   Mark dislikes whomever John likes.
   John likes Sally, but not Daryl.
   Mark likes Daryl, but not Sally.

   A) True
   B) False
   C) Not certain

Numerical Series and Sequences

19) What is the next number in the following sequence? 1, 5, 9, 13, 17, . . .

   A) 20
   B) 21
   C) 30
   D) 40

Analogies of Place

20) Captain is to ship as:
   A) Car is to mechanic
   B) Chef is to kitchen
   C) Worship is to temple
   D) Tent is to teepee

Smallest Multiple of a Number

21) A cafeteria serves spaghetti to senior citizens on Fridays. The spaghetti comes prepared in large containers, and each container holds 15 servings of spaghetti. The cafeteria is expecting 82 senior citizens this Friday. What is the least number of containers of spaghetti that the cafeteria will need in order to serve all 82 people?
   A) 4
   B) 5
   C) 6
   D) 7

Identifying Synonyms

22) Insuperable nearly means the same as:
   A) indiscriminate
   B) impassable
   C) incredible
   D) indomitable

Rate, Time, and Distance

23) A worm crawls 10.5 inches in 45 seconds. How far will it travel in 6 minutes?

   A) 45 inches
   B) 63 inches
   C) 64 inches
   D) 84 inches

Visual Data Representations

24) The pictograph below shows the number of pizzas sold in one day at a local pizzeria. Cheese pizzas sold for $10 each, pepperoni pizzas sold for $12, and the total sales of all three types of pizza was $310. What is the sales price of one vegetable pizza?

Cheese	▼ ▼ ▼
Pepperoni	▼ ▼
Vegetable	▼

Each ▼ represents 5 pizzas.

   A) $5
   B) $8
   C) $9
   D) $10

Identifying Synonyms – Further Questions

25) <u>Terse</u> means the same as:
    A) exempt
    B) tense
    C) abrupt
    D) principled

Finding the Missing Value in the Calculation of an Average

26) The ages of 5 siblings are: 2, 5, 7, 12, and x. If the mean age of the 5 siblings is 8 years old, what is the age of the 5th sibling?
    A) 8
    B) 10
    C) 12
    D) 14

Finding the Missing Word in a Proverb – Further Questions

27) People who live in glass _____ shouldn't throw stones.
    A) mansions
    B) houses
    C) castles
    D) prisons

Working with Fractional Values

28) If $\frac{x}{24}$ is between 8 and 9, which of the following could be the value of *x*?

A) 190

B) 191

C) 200

D) 217

Forming Words from Anagrams

29) Unscramble the letters to form an English word:

U U U A L N S

Ordering Numbers from Least to Greatest

30) Which of the following shows the numbers ordered from least to greatest?

A) 0.2135
0.3152
0.0253
0.0012

B) 0.3152
0.2135
0.0253
0.0012

C) 0.0253
0.0012
0.3152
0.2135

D) 0.0012
    0.0253
    0.2135
    0.3152

Understanding Antonyms

31) <u>Amplify</u> is the opposite of:
    A) magnify
    B) diminish
    C) lengthen
    D) extend

Rearranging Words to Form a Sentence – Further Questions

32) Rearrange the following words to form a sentence:

    most opinion flowers are daisies my in beautiful the

Calculating Fractional Parts of a Whole

33) At the beginning of class, $1/5$ of the students leave to go to singing lessons. Then $1/4$ of the remaining students leave to go to the principal's office. If 18 students are then left in the class, how many students were there at the beginning of class?
    A) 90
    B) 45
    C) 30
    D) 25

Identifying Duplicates in Lists of Letters with Punctuation

34) How many of the pairs below are duplicates?

Grindlewon, M.N.	Grindlewon, M.N.
Donjohnson, L O	Donjohnson, L. O
Kistrerfang, PJ.	Kistrerfang, PJ
Longferwort. LK	Longferwort. LK
Unhunderten, SR,	Unhunderten, SR.

Math Word Problems with Multiple Operations – Further Questions

35) An after-school class had 100 students at the beginning of January. It lost 15% of its students during the month. However, 15 new students joined the class on the last day of the month. If this pattern continues for the next two months, how many students will there be in the class at the end of March?
   A) 185
   B) 100
   C) 110
   D) 115

Calculating Discounted Prices

36) The price of a wool coat is reduced 12.5% at the end of the winter. If the original price of the coat was $120, what will the price be after the reduction?
   A) $108.00
   B) $107.50
   C) $105.70
   D) $105.00

Identifying the Word That is Different from the Group – Adjectives

37) Which word below is most different to the others?

   Beautiful

   Magnificent

   Lovely

   Inauspicious

   Relaxing

Analysis of Geometric Figures in a Series

38) If the pattern continues, which figure will be next in the sequence?

A)

B)

C)

D)

Distance Traveled and Miles per Hour

39) A motorcycle traveled 38.4 miles in $4/5$ of an hour. What was the approximate speed of the motorcycle in miles per hour?

   A) 9.6
   B) 30.72
   C) 48
   D) 52

Ratios and Proportions

40) A factory that makes microchips produces 20 times as many functioning chips as defective chips. If the factory produced 11,235 chips in total last week, how many of them were defective?

   A) 535
   B) 561
   C) 1,070
   D) 10,700

Greatest Multiple of a Number – Further Questions

41) A town has recently suffered a flood. In order to accommodate the residents in emergency housing, the town will pay $2,550 in up-front costs. It will then need to pay $750 for each resident that it accommodates. If the town has a total of $55,000 available immediately after the flood, what is the greatest number of residents that it can house?

   A) 68
   B) 69
   C) 70
   D) 71

Quick Identification of Months and Dates

42) The tenth month of the year is:
   1) August
   2) October
   3) September
   4) November
   5) July

Finding the Product of Two Numbers

43) What is the largest possible product of two even integers whose sum is 30?
   A) 14
   B) 16
   C) 210
   D) 224

Understanding the Relationship Between Two Words – Further Questions

44) Which phrase below best describes the relationship between these two words:

   IMPLICATE   EXONERATE

   A) They have similar meanings.
   B) They have contradictory meanings.
   C) They have unrelated meanings.

Calculating *Percentage Discounts*

45) The price of a certain book is reduced from $60 to $45 at the end of the semester. By what percent is the price of the book reduced?
   A) 15%
   B) 20%
   C) 25%
   D) 33%

Analogies of Cause and Effect

46) Germ is to contaminate as:
   A) Injury is to heal
   B) Break is to bone
   C) Insubordination is to sloth
   D) Debt is to bankrupt

Profit and Mark-Up of Cost

47) A company buys an item at a cost of B and sells it at five times the cost. Which of the following represents the profit made on each item?
   A) B
   B) 4B
   C) 5B
   D) 5 – B

Understanding Antonyms – Further Questions

48)   Inchoate is the opposite of:
    A) rudimentary
    B) developed
    C) amorphous
    D) incipient

Following Instructions to Form a 3-D Figure

49)   By following which set of directions below will a cube be formed?

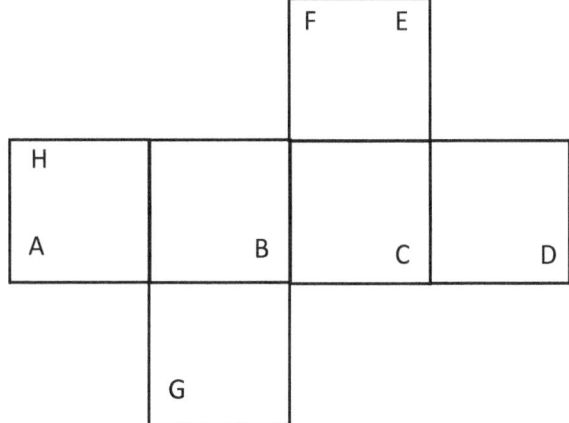

    A) Fold corner A to corner D, corner G to corner D, and corner E to corner H.
    B) Fold corner A to corner D, corner G to corner H, and corner F to corner H.
    C) Fold corner A to corner D, corner H to corner D, and corner F to corner G.
    D) Fold corner A to corner H, corner G to corner D, and corner F to corner H.

Identifying Synonyms – Further Questions

50) Extortionate means the same as:

   A) expressive
   B) exorbitant
   C) excusable
   D) exclusive

WONDERLIC SLE PRACTICE TEST 2

1) 4.25 + 0.003 + 0.148 = ?
   A) 4.401
   B) 4.428
   C) 5.76
   D) 44.01

2) Unscramble the letters to form an English word:

   K N N N W O U

3) If $7x$ is between 5 and 6, which of the following could be the value of x?
   A) ²/₃
   B) ³/₄
   C) ⁵/₈
   D) ⁷/₈

4) Keep your friends close and your _____ closer.
   A) besties
   B) relatives
   C) enemies
   D) family

5) The temperature on Saturday was 62° F at 5:00 PM and 38° F at 11:00 PM. If the temperature fell at a constant rate on Saturday, what was the temperature at 9:00 PM?
   A) 58° F
   B) 54° F
   C) 50° F
   D) 46° F

6) <u>Superlative</u> is the opposite of:
   A) top-notch
   B) inferior
   C) exclusive
   D) excellent

7) A painter needs to paint 8 rooms, each of which have a surface area of 2000 square feet. If one bucket of paint covers 900 square feet, what is the fewest number of buckets of paint that must be used to complete all 8 rooms?
   A) 3
   B) 17
   C) 18
   D) 19

8) <u>Culminate</u> means the same as:
   A) impart
   B) correct
   C) conclude
   D) appeal

9) Bryony jogged 3.6 miles in $3/4$ of an hour. What was her average jogging speed in miles per hour?
   A) 2.7
   B) 4.0
   C) 4.2
   D) 4.8

10) The ratio of males to females in the senior year class of Carson Heights High School was 6 to 7. If the total number of students in the class is 117, how many males are in the class?

A) 48
B) 54
C) 56
D) 58

11) A picture is worth a thousand _____ .

A) comments
B) remarks
C) dollars
D) words

12) A student receives the following scores on his exams during the semester: 89, 65, 75, 68, 82, 74, 86. What is the mean of his scores?

A) 24
B) 74
C) 75
D) 77

13) A field is 100 yards long and 32 yards wide. What is the area of the field in square yards? (Area of a square or rectangle: length × width)

A) 160
B) 320
C) 1600
D) 3200

14) The triangle in the illustration below is an isosceles triangle which has two sides of equal length. If angle A is 32 degrees, what is the measurement of angle B?

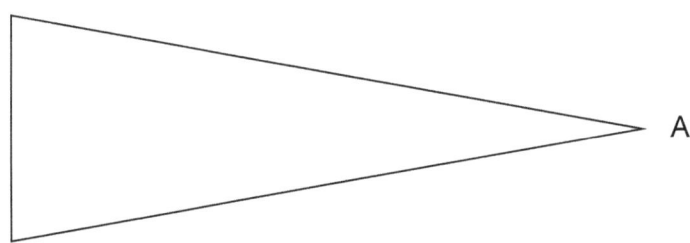

A) 32°
B) 45°
C) 74°
D) 148°

15) Assume the first two statements are true. Is the third one also true?

All members must sign the register today.
He did not sign the register today.
He is not a member.

A) True
B) False
C) Not certain

16) What is the perimeter of a rectangle that has a length of 17 and a width of 4?
perimeter formula: (length × 2) + (width × 2)

A) 21
B) 34
C) 42
D) 68

17) Magnanimous is the opposite of:
   A) diplomatic
   B) altruistic
   C) uncharitable
   D) unselfish

18) The table below shows information on disease by different types. Approximately how many cancer and leukemia patients have not survived?

Disease or Complication	Percentage of patients of this disease or complication type that have survived and total number of patients
Cardiopulmonary and vascular	82% (602,000)
HIV/AIDS	73% (215,000)
Diabetes	89% (793,000)
Cancer and leukemia	48% (231,000)
Premature birth complications	64% (68,000)

   A) 24,480
   B) 110,880
   C) 120,120
   D) 231,000

19) Sublime means nearly the same as:
   A) acceptable
   B) superb
   C) baleful
   D) lowly

20) The ratio of bags of carrots to bags of potatoes in a certain grocery store is 1 to 4. If there are 44 bags of carrots in the store, how many bags of potatoes are there?
   A) 11
   B) 22
   C) 33
   D) 176

21) Ingenious is to idea as:
   A) Uneducated is to ignorance
   B) Stupidity is to knowledge
   C) Artistic is to untalented
   D) Skillful is to clumsy

22) There are three boys in a family, named Greg, Matt, and William. Greg is three years older than twice the age of William. If Greg is 10 years old and Matt is 16 years old, how old is William?
   A) 35
   B) 23
   C) 5
   D) 2

23) Rearrange the following words to form a sentence:

   include favorite reading swimming hobbies his and

24) 90 is 30 percent of what number?
   A) 27
   B) 120
   C) 0.0375
   D) 300

25) How many of the pairs below are duplicates?

#@!*&6543	#@!*&6543
<,) G ^ 987	<.) G ^ 987
BN$@#"361	BN$@#'361
(*&! LB145	(*&! LB145
= : + * 964V	= ; + * 964V

26) A local club has 31 members. If each member contributes 12 cans of food for a food drive, how many cans of food are contributed in total?
   A) 472
   B) 372
   C) 132
   D) 43

27) Which word below is most different to the others?

   Driveway

   Vehicle

   Road

   Highway

   Path

28) Convert the following fraction to decimal format: $5/50$
   A) 0.0010
   B) 0.0100
   C) 0.1000
   D) 0.0500

29) It is January now and Isabelle has just gotten engaged. She is going to get married in 18 months. In what month is she going to get married?
   A) August
   B) July
   C) September
   D) June

30) Mary needs to get $650 in donations. So far, she has obtained 80% of the money she needs. How much money does she still need?
   A) $8.19
   B) $13.00
   C) $32.50
   D) $130.00

31) Which phrase below best describes the relationship between these two words:

   GENIAL   ADROIT

   A) They have similar meanings.
   B) They have contradictory meanings.
   C) They have unrelated meanings.

32) A baseball team had 50 games this season and lost 20 percent of them. How many games did the team win?
   A) 8
   B) 10
   C) 20
   D) 40

33) Rearrange the following words to form a sentence:

   he black a karate has belt in

34) Marcos can run 3 miles in 25 minutes. If he maintains this pace, how long will it take him to run 12 miles?
   A) 1 hour and 15 minutes
   B) 1 hour and 40 minutes
   C) 1 hour and 45 minutes
   D) 3 hours

35) Money is to bank as:
   A) Bake is to potato
   B) Plant is to tree
   C) Foot is to shoe
   D) Garden is to fertilizer

36) Find the value that solves the following proportion: $9/6 = ?/10$
   A) 1.5
   B) 15
   C) .67
   D) 67

37) How many of the pairs below are duplicates?

   JAICNCYATSD   JAICNGYATSD

   HSIWNCIAG   HSIWNCIAG

   LAOCNAGSUQ   LAOCNAGSUQ

   KLINAMVSNAL   KLINAMVNSAL

   PYTCVXSTASM   PYTCVXSATSM

38) In a high school, 17 out of every 20 students participate in a sport. If there are 800 students at the high school, what is the total number of students that participate in a sport?

A) 120 students
B) 640 students
C) 680 students
D) 776 students

39) Which phrase below best describes the relationship between these two words:

COLOSSAL   MINISCULE

A) They have similar meanings.
B) They have contradictory meanings.
C) They have unrelated meanings.

40) There are 10 cars in a parking lot. Nine of the cars are 2, 3, 4, 5, 6, 7, 9, 10, and 12 years old, respectively. If the average age of the 10 cars is 6 years old, how old is the 10th car?

A) 1 year old
B) 2 years old
C) 3 years old
D) 4 years old

41) Assume the first two statements are true. Is the third one also true?

People who wear eyeglasses are intelligent.
She is intelligent.
She wears eyeglasses.

A) True
B) False
C) Not certain

42) A dance judge awards a number from 1 to 10 to score dancers during a TV show. During one show, he judged five dancers and awarded the following scores: 9.9, 9.9, 8.2, 7.6 and 6.8. What was the average of his scores for this show?

A) 8.2
B) 8.48
C) 9.9
D) 3.1

43) Which proverb is most similar to the one below?

Fight fire with fire.

A) A leopard doesn't change its spots.
B) Better the devil you know.
C) An eye for an eye, a tooth for a tooth.
D) Keep your nose to the grindstone.

44) A rectangular box has a base that is 5 inches wide and 6 inches long. The height of the box is 10 inches. What is the volume of the box?
(Box volume = length × width × height.)

A) 30
B) 110
C) 150
D) 300

45) Which word below is most different to the others?

Carrot

Steak

Fork

Candy

Bread

46) Four members of a family are having a meal in a restaurant. They each have a main dish and a desert. The main dishes are all the same price each, and the deserts are also all the same price for each dessert. The main dishes cost $8 each. The total cost of their meal is $48. How much did each of their deserts cost?
A) $3.75
B) $4
C) $6
D) $22

47) Pernicious means the same as:
A) advantageous
B) benevolent
C) dangerous
D) obnoxious

48) The term BPM, heartbeats per minute, measures how many heartbeats a person has every 60 seconds. To calculate BPM, the heartbeat is taken for ten seconds, represented by variable B. Which one of the following is used to calculate BPM?
A) BPM ÷ 60
B) BPM ÷ 10
C) B6
D) B10

49) The ideal BPM of a healthy person is 60. Which of the following is used to calculate by how much a person's BPM exceeds the ideal BPM?
A) 60 + BPM
B) 60 − BPM
C) BPM + 60
D) BPM − 60

50) Shrimp is to seafood as:
A) Sweet is to cake
B) Water is to lake
C) Trout is to fish
D) Eat is to meal

WONDERLIC SLE PRACTICE TEST 3

1) A fuel tanker truck has a capacity of 1200 gallons. If it takes 75 minutes to fill the tanker truck, at what rate is it being filled?

   A) 6.25 gallons per minute
   B) 16 gallons per minute
   C) 62.5 gallons per minute
   D) 160 gallons per minute

2) Which phrase below best describes the relationship between these two words:

   RETICENT   GARRULOUS

   A) They have similar meanings.
   B) They have contradictory meanings.
   C) They have unrelated meanings.

3) An employee at the Department of Motor Vehicles wanted to find the mean of the ten driving theory tests they administered this morning. However, the employee divided the total points from the ten tests by 8, which gave him an erroneous result of 78. What is the correct mean of the ten tests?

   A) 97.5
   B) 70
   C) 62.4
   D) 52

4) Yesterday a train traveled $117^3/_4$ miles. Today it traveled $102^1/_6$ miles. What is the difference between the distance traveled today and yesterday?

   A) 15 miles
   B) $15^1/_4$ miles
   C) $15^7/_{12}$ miles
   D) $15^9/_{12}$ miles

5) Ski is to snow as:
   A) Sun is to tan
   B) Beach is to ocean
   C) Rain is to flood
   D) Swim is to water

6) Sam is driving a truck at 70 miles per hour. At 10:30 am, he sees this sign:

Brownsville	35 miles
Dunnstun	70 miles
Farnam	140 miles
Georgetown	210 miles

   After Sam sees the sign, he continues to drive at the same speed. At 11:00 am, how far will he be from Farnam?
   A) He will be in Farnam.
   B) He will be 35 miles from Farnam.
   C) He will be 70 miles from Farnam.
   D) He will be 105 miles from Farnam.

7) Rearrange the following words to form a sentence:

   the are you work likely succeed more harder the you to

8) In a math class, $1/3$ of the students fail a test. If twelve students have failed the test, how many students are in the class in total?
   A) 15
   B) 16
   C) 36
   D) 38

9) Beauty is in the eye of the _____ .
   A) beloved
   B) bejeweled
   C) bewitched
   D) beholder

10) Mark owns a bargain bookstore that sells every book for $5. Last week, his sales were $525. This week his sales figure was $600. How many more books did Mark sell this week, compared to last week?
    A) 5
    B) 15
    C) 25
    D) 75

11) Kieko needs to calculate 16% of 825. Which of the following should she use?
    A) 825 × 16
    B) 160 × 825
    C) 825 × 1600
    D) 825 × 0.16

12) Charlie got her first treatment in February. She needs to wait 6 months to get her second treatment. In what month will Charlie get her second treatment?
    A) September
    B) October
    C) August
    D) June

13) Wei Lei bought a shirt on sale. The original price of the shirt was $18, and he got a 40% discount. What was the sales price of the shirt?
   A) $7.20
   B) $10.80
   C) $11.80
   D) $17.60

14) If the pattern continues, which figure will be next in the sequence?

A)

B)

C)

D)

15) The county is proposing a 7.5% increase in its annual real estate tax. If the tax is currently $480 per year, how much would the tax be if the proposed increase is approved?
   A) $444
   B) $487
   C) $516
   D) $840

16) Which word below is most different to the others?

   Friendship

   Peace

   Prosperity

   Hardship

   Success

17) Mrs. Ramirez is inviting 12 children to her son's birthday party. The children will play pin the tail on the donkey. Mrs. Ramirez has already made 40 tails for the game. She wants to give each child 4 tails to play the game. How many more tails does she need to make?
   A) 4
   B) 8
   C) 10
   D) 12

18) The squeaky _____ gets the grease.
   A) wheel
   B) hinge
   C) door
   D) handle

19) A class contains 20 students. On Tuesday 5% of the students were absent. On Wednesday 20% of the students were absent. How many more students were absent on Wednesday than on Tuesday?
   A) 1
   B) 2
   C) 3
   D) 4

20) Which phrase below best describes the relationship between these two words:

   CATALYST   IMPETUS

   A) They have similar meanings.
   B) They have contradictory meanings.
   C) They have unrelated meanings.

21) Records indicate that there were 12 hospitals in Johnson County in 1998, but this number had increased to 15 hospitals in 2020. There were 12 births per hospital in Johnson County in 1998. The total number of births in Johnson County was 240 in 2020. By what amount does the average number of births per hospital in Johnson County for 2020 exceed those for 1998?
   A) 3 births per hospital
   B) 4 births per hospital
   C) 15 births per hospital
   D) 16 births per hospital

22) Unscramble the letters to form an English word:

F J S T I U Y

23) ABC is an isosceles triangle. Angle DAC is 109° and points A, B, and D are co-linear. What is the measurement of ∠C?

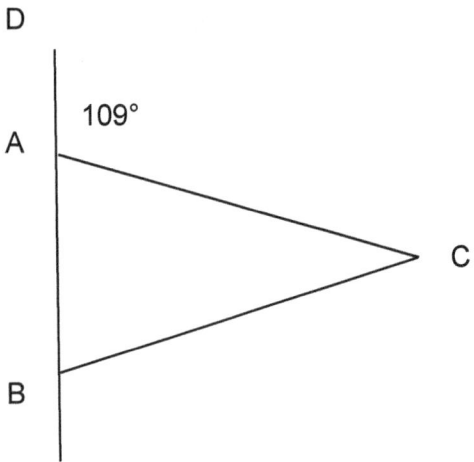

A) 71°
B) 38°
C) 138°
D) 180°

24) Rearrange the following words to form a sentence:

really very person she a kind is

25) Denisha can walk one mile in 17 minutes. At this rate, how long would it take her to walk 5 miles?
   A) 1 hour and 5 minutes
   B) 1 hour and 7 minutes
   C) 1 hour and 8 minutes
   D) 1 hour and 25 minutes

26) Bart is riding his bike at a rate of 12 miles per hour. He arrives in the town of Wilmington at 3:00 pm. The town of Mount Pleasant is 50 miles from Wilmington. How far will Bart be from Mount Pleasant at 5:00 pm if he continues riding his bike at this speed?
   A) 12 miles
   B) 20 miles
   C) 24 miles
   D) 26 miles

27) Fabric is to clothing as:
   A) Bird is to nest
   B) Tennis is to court
   C) Milk is to cheese
   D) Work is to money

28) A ticket office sold 360 more tickets on Friday than it did on Saturday. If the office sold 2570 tickets in total during Friday and Saturday, how many tickets did it sell on Friday?
   A) 360
   B) 1105
   C) 1465
   D) 1565

29) How many of the pairs below are duplicates?

Fiztpackrick, Emerson	Fitzpactrick, Emerson
Jefferys, Kimberly	Jeffereys, Kimberly
Hindmens, Johanes	Hindmens, Johnanes
Eldeberg, Matilda	Elderberg, Matilda
Valdervon, Dakota	Valdervon, Dakota

30) Tom's height increased by 10% this year. If Tom was 5 feet tall at the beginning of the year, how tall is he now?
   A) 5 feet 1 inch
   B) 5 feet 5 inches
   C) 5 feet 6 inches
   D) 5 feet 10 inches

31) Assume the first two statements are true. Is the third one also true?

Eating chocolate makes dogs ill.
My dog has just eaten chocolate.
My dog will become ill.

   A) True
   B) False
   C) Not certain

32) Jason does the high jump for his high school track and field team. His first jump is at 3.246 meters. His second is 3.331 meters, and his third is 3.328 meters. If the height of each jump is rounded up or down to the nearest one-hundredth of a meter (also called a centimeter), what is the estimate of the total height for all three jumps combined?
A) 9.80
B) 9.89
C) 9.90
D) 9.91

33) Beleaguer is the opposite of:
A) beset
B) plague
C) annoy
D) placate

34) Use the table below to answer the question that follows.

Regional Railway Train Service	
Departure Time	Arrival Time
9:50 am	10:36 am
11:15 am	12:01 pm
12:30 pm	1:16 pm
2:15 pm	3:01 pm
?	5:51 pm

The journey on the Regional Railway is always exactly the same duration.
What is the missing time in the chart above?
A) 3:30 pm
B) 4:15 pm
C) 4:30 pm
D) 5:05 pm

35) Which word below is most different to the others?

Shopping

Swimming

Cleaning

Traveling

Gaming

36) Captain Smith needs to purchase rope for his fleet of yachts. He owns 26 yachts and needs 6 feet 10 inches of rope for each one. How much rope does he need in total?
   A) 152 feet
   B) 177 feet 8 inches
   C) 257 feet 8 inches
   D) 260 feet

37) <u>Inculcate</u> means the same as:
   A) brainwash
   B) neglect
   C) cultivate
   D) concur

38) Find the value that solves the following proportion: $3/6 = ?/14$
   A) 3
   B) 6
   C) 7
   D) 8

39) Disappointment is to expectation as:

A) Courage is to fear

B) Touch is to smell

C) Faith is to joy

D) Desperation is to hope

40) The illustration below shows the number of traffic violations that occur every week in a certain city. The fine for speeding violations is $50 per violation. The fine for other violations is $20 per violation. The total collected for all three types of violations was $6,000. What is the fine for each parking violation?

Speeding	☆ ☆
Parking	☆
Other violations	☆ ☆ ☆

Each ☆ represents 30 violations.

A) $20

B) $30

C) $40

D) $100

41) Which proverb is most similar to the one below?

A bird in the hand is worth two in the bush.

A) Make hay while the sun shines.

B) Kill two birds with one stone.

C) Don't put all of your eggs in one basket.

D) Half a loaf is better than none.

42) Davina is using a recipe that requires 2 cups of sugar for every one-third cup of butter. If she uses 12 cups of sugar, how many cups of butter should she use?
   A) 6 cups of butter
   B) 3 cups of butter
   C) 2 cups of butter
   D) $\frac{1}{3}$ cup of butter

43) Abscond nearly means the same as:
   A) give up
   B) loathe
   C) remain
   D) disappear

44) A driver travels at 60 miles per hour for two and a half hours before her car fails to start at a service station. She has to wait two hours while the car is repaired before she can continue driving. She then drives at 75 miles an hour for the remainder of her journey. She is traveling to Denver, and her journey is 240 miles in total. If she left home at 6:00 am, what time will she arrive in Denver?
   A) 9:30 am
   B) 11:30 am
   C) 11:42 am
   D) 11:50 am

45) Redundant is the opposite of:
   A) otiose
   B) superfluous
   C) useful
   D) necessary

46) A clothing store sells jackets and jeans at a discount during a sales period. The total amount of money the store collected for sales of jeans and jackets during the sales period was $4,000. The amount of money earned from selling jackets was one-third of that earned from selling jeans. The jeans sold for $20 a pair. How many pairs of jeans did the store sell during the sales period?

A) 15
B) 20
C) 150
D) 200

47) Assume the first two statements are true. Is the third one also true?

Sufferers of malaria have a fever.
He has a fever.
He suffers from malaria.

A) True
B) False
C) Not certain

48) Milk fills a tank at a diary at a rate of 3.5 gallons per minute. If the tank has a 500-gallon capacity, approximately how long will it take to fill the tank?

A) 2 hours and 23 minutes
B) 2 hours and 13 minutes
C) 1 hour and 43 minutes
D) 1 hour and 42 minutes

49) Dig is to shovel as:
   A) Spoon is to plate
   B) Hammer is to nail
   C) Cut is to scissors
   D) Summer is to season

50) How many of the pairs below are duplicates?

Wallerson, N.I.	Wallersen, N.I.
Neilson, G.K.	Neillson, G.K.
Trumann, A.P.	Trumann, A.P.
Pina, Q.Y.	Pino, G.Y.
Zumbolt, B.N.	Zumbolt, B.N.

WONDERLIC SLE PRACTICE TEST 4

1) Scholarly is to academic as:
   A) Penury is to affluence
   B) Deleterious is to beneficial
   C) Intelligent is to clever
   D) Money is to income

2) What number is next in this sequence? 2, 4, 8, 16
   A) 18
   B) 20
   C) 24
   D) 32

3) Assume the first two statements are true. Is the third one also true?

   Eating whole-grain products is good for you.
   That bread is good for you.
   That bread is a whole-grain product.

   A) True
   B) False
   C) Not certain

4) It takes Martha 4 hours and 10 minutes to knit one woolen cap. At this rate, how long will it take her to knit 12 caps?
   A) 40 hours
   B) 42 hours
   C) 46 hours
   D) 50 hours

5) Which phrase below best describes the relationship between these two words:

PROCLIVITY   PREDELICTION

A) They have similar meanings.
B) They have contradictory meanings.
C) They have unrelated meanings.

6) The Jones family needs to dig a new well. The well will be 525 feet deep, and it will be topped with a windmill which will be 95 feet in height. What is the distance from the deepest point of the well to the top of the windmill?
A) 95 feet
B) 430 feet
C) 525 feet
D) 620 feet

7) How many of the pairs below are duplicates?

1200967801	1200967801
4523901423	4523901423
9876123462	9876123462
3716920163	3719620163
7152629102	7125629102

8) A store is offering a 15% discount on backpacks. Janet's purchase would be $90 at the normal price. How much will she pay after the discount?
A) $75.50
B) $76.50
C) $77.50
D) $85.50

9) <u>Winsome</u> means the same as:
   A) talkative
   B) wholesome
   C) attractive
   D) divine

10) John is measuring plant growth as part of a botany experiment. Last week, his plant grew 7¾ inches, but this week his plant grew 10½ inches. What is the difference in growth in inches between the two weeks?
   A) 2¼ inches
   B) 2½ inches
   C) 2¾ inches
   D) 3¼ inches

11) Rearrange the following words to form a sentence:

   business year there than ever more this are students before

12) Patty works 23 hours a week at a part time job for which she receives $7.50 an hour. She then gets a raise, after which she earns $184 per week. She continues to work 23 hours per week. How much did her hourly pay increase?
   A) 50 cents an hour
   B) 75 cents an hour
   C) $1.00 an hour
   D) $8.00 an hour

13) Which word below is most different to the others?

Students

Teachers

Librarians

Administrators

Professors

14) Sheng Li is driving at 70 miles per hour. At 10:00 am, he sees this sign:

Washington	140 miles
Yorkville	105 miles
Zorster	210 miles

He continues driving at the same speed. Where will Sheng Li be at 11:00 am?

A) 70 miles from Washington

B) 105 miles from Washington

C) 75 miles from Yorkville

D) 80 miles from Yorkville

15) Kevin started a diet four months ago. It is now August and he has lost 30 pounds. In what month did he start his diet?

A) May

B) June

C) April

D) December

16) Mayumi spent the day counting cars for her job as a traffic controller. In the morning she counted 114 more cars than she did in the afternoon. If she counted 300 cars in total that day, how many cars did she count in the morning?
   A) 90
   B) 93
   C) 114
   D) 207

17) Revile means the same as:
   A) approach
   B) reproach
   C) approve
   D) exonerate

18) Item C costs 20% more per pound than item B. If a 12-pound container of item B costs $48, what is the cost per pound of item C?
   A) $4.12
   B) $4.20
   C) $4.60
   D) $4.80

19) Heal is to wound as:
   A) Mend is to break
   B) Heat is to fireplace
   C) Labrador is to dog
   D) Job is to work

20) The cost of a photography course is $20 per week plus a $5 fee per week for review of photographs and administration. What is the total cost of the course and fees for W weeks?

   A) $20W
   B) $25W
   C) $20 + 5W
   D) $5 + 20W

21) Which phrase below best describes the relationship between these two words:

   IMPECCABLE   IMPECUNIOUS

   A) They have similar meanings.
   B) They have contradictory meanings.
   C) They have unrelated meanings.

22) Which of the following shows the numbers ordered from least to greatest?

   A) $-1/4, 1/8, 1/6, 1$
   B) $-1/4, 1/8, 1, 1/6$
   C) $-1/4, 1/6, 1/8, 1$
   D) $-1/4, 1, 1/8, 1/6$

23) Assume the first two statements are true. Is the third one also true?

   Declaring bankruptcy is a common civil procedure in court.
   She works in the court house.
   She deals with those declaring bankruptcy.

   A) True
   B) False
   C) Not certain

24) The graph below shows the relationship between the total number of hamburgers a restaurant sells and the total sales in dollars for the hamburgers. The cost of shakes, where c is the cost and s is the number of shakes, is represented by: $c = \frac{9}{4}s$. Which of the following best estimates difference between the cost of one hamburger and the cost of one shake?

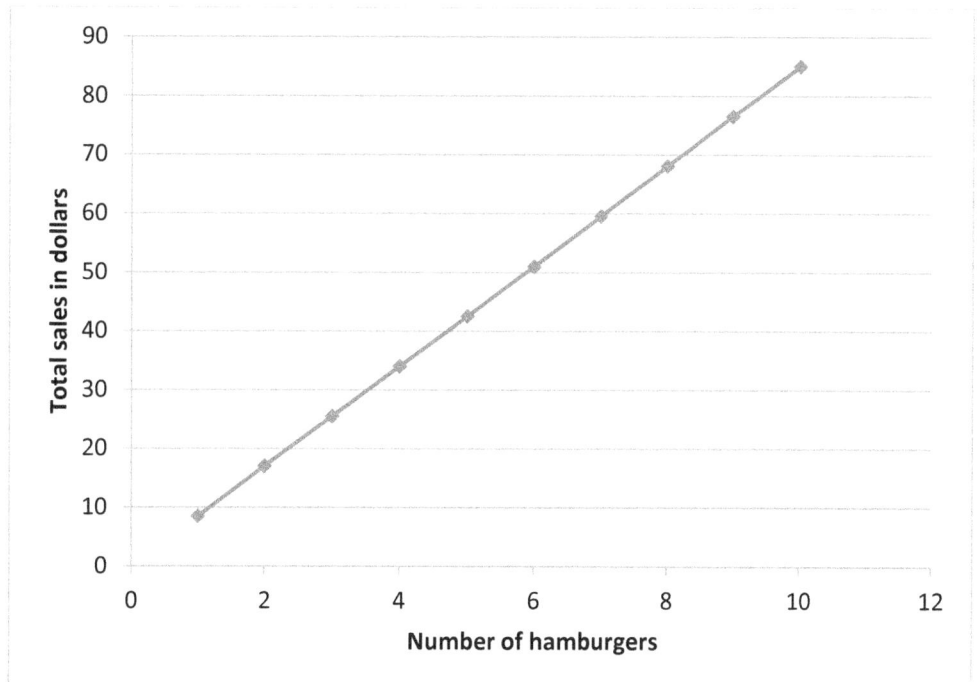

A) $2.25
B) $4.25
C) $6.25
D) $8.20

25) <u>Lassitude</u> means the same as:
A) diligence
B) liveliness
C) exhaustion
D) satisfaction

26) What is 12.86749 rounded to the nearest tenth?
   A) 10
   B) 12
   C) 12.87
   D) 12.9

27) How many of the pairs below are duplicates?

   WATERFULL   WATERFUL

   AMAZODON   AMAZADON

   QUESTNET   QUESTNET

   NEEDLOG   NEEDGOL

   DULLDUM   DULLDUM

28) Point B is at 0.35 on a number line and the distance between point B and point C is 1.2. Which of the following could be the location of point C?
   A) 0.23
   B) 0.47
   C) −0.85
   D) 0.85

29) Rearrange the following words to form a sentence:

   headache eating give ice you too cream quickly can a

30) What is the sum of 15.845 + 8.21 to the nearest integer?
   A) 24.055
   B) 24
   C) 23
   D) 22

31) Which word below is most different to the others?

Lacerate

Injure

Burn

Prepare

Sprain

32) At an elementary school, 3 out of ten students are taking an art class. If the school has 650 students in total, how many total students are taking an art class?
A) 65
B) 130
C) 195
D) 217

33) Bird is to flock as:
A) Sheep is to herd
B) Cow is to field
C) Dog is to pet
D) Animal is to human

34) Which of the following is the greatest?
A) .540
B) .054
C) .045
D) .5045

35) Never look a _____ horse in the mouth.
   A) lame
   B) gift
   C) dead
   D) tired

36) An athlete ran 10 miles in 1.5 hours. The graph below shows the miles the athlete ran every 10 minutes. According to the graph, how many miles did the athlete run in the first 30 minutes?

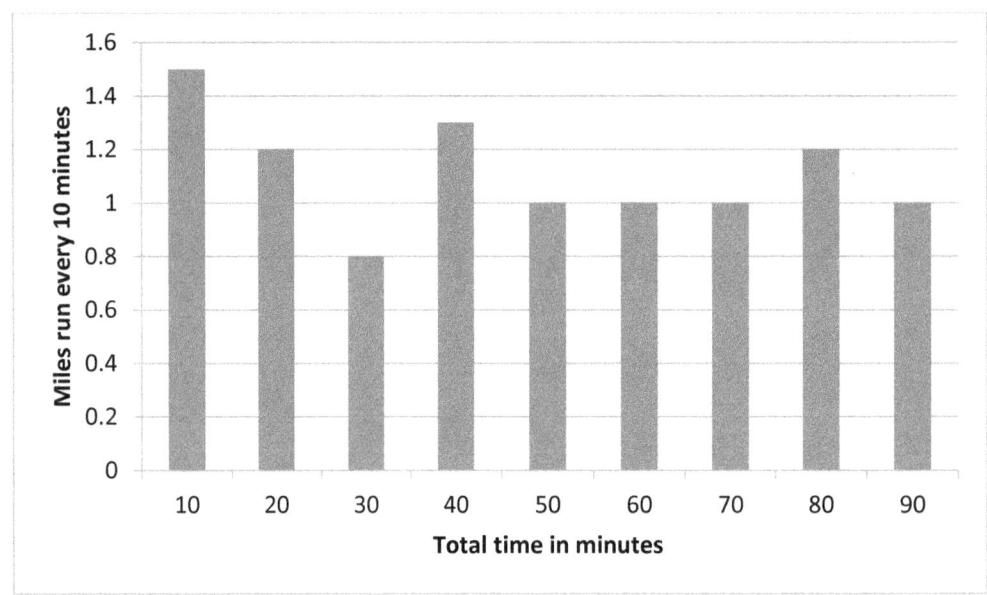

   A) 0.8 miles
   B) 2.0 miles
   C) 3.0 miles
   D) 3.5 miles

37) Accost is the opposite of:
   A) accept
   B) confront
   C) regret
   D) shun

38) Martin is using a plaster mix to repair a wall in his house. The instructions for the mix state that 3 ounces of water should be added for every 4 ounces of plaster pounder used. If he uses 14 ounces of plaster powder, how much water should he add?

A) 56 ounces of water

B) 41 ounces of water

C) 10.5 ounces of water

D) 3 ounces of water

39) Console is the opposite of:

A) encourage

B) sympathize

C) antagonize

D) rebel

40) What is the next number in the following sequence? 2, 6, 18, 54, . . .

A) 60

B) 72

C) 80

D) 162

41) Dexterous means the same as:

A) adroit

B) awkward

C) inept

D) convenient

42) Mount Pleasant is 15,138 feet high. Mount Glacier is 9,927 feet high. What is the best estimate of the difference between the altitudes of the two mountains to the nearest thousand feet?

A) 5,000
B) 4,000
C) 6,000
D) 25,000

43) Yesterday the temperature was 90 degrees. Today it is 10% cooler than yesterday. What is today's temperature?

A) 70 degrees
B) 71 degrees
C) 80 degrees
D) 81 degrees

44) Unscramble the letters to form an English word:

C A C E T P

45) Ranvir started the day with 15½ pies for sale in her bakery. She ended the day with 2¼ pies. If no pies were added or removed during the day, how may pies did she sell this day?

A) 12¼
B) 12¾
C) 13¼
D) 13¾

46) By following which set of directions below will a cube be formed?

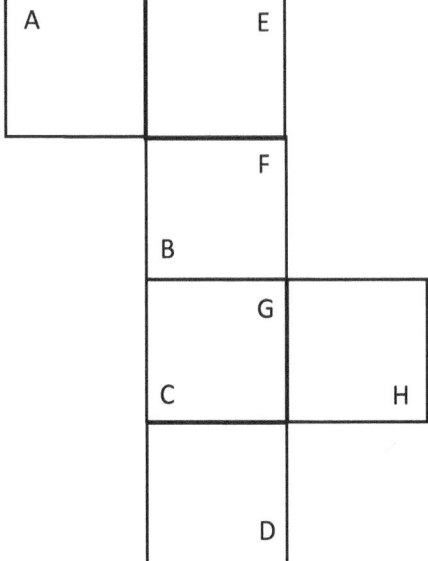

A) Fold corner D to corner E, corner A to corner B, and corner H to corner F.
B) Fold corner D to corner E, corner A to corner D, and corner H to corner F.
C) Fold corner D to corner E, corner A to corner C, and corner H to corner F.
D) Fold corner D to corner E, corner A to corner C, and corner H to corner E.

47) $2/10$ is equivalent to what percentage?
A) 10%
B) 20%
C) 25%
D) 50%

48) At the beginning of a class, one-fourth of the students leave to attend band practice. Later, one half of the remaining students leave to go to PE. If there were 15 students remaining in the class at the end, how many students were in the class at the beginning?
   A) 20
   B) 25
   C) 35
   D) 40

49) There's no such thing as a free _____ .
   A) lunch
   B) ticket
   C) ride
   D) loan

50) Tom bought a phone on sale for $120. The original price of the phone was $150. What was the percentage of the discount on the sale?
   A) 10%
   B) 20%
   C) 25%
   D) 30%

ANSWER KEY

Wonderlic SLE Practice Test 1

1) B

2) A

3) A

4) 3

5) A

6) B

7) C

8) A

9) B

10) D

11) A

12) A rolling stone gathers no moss.

13) A

14) farmer

15) D

16) C

17) A

18) C

19) B

20) B

21) C

22) B

23) D

24) B

25) C

© COPYRIGHT 2017, 2020 Exam SAM Study Aids & Media dba www.examsam.com
This material may not be copied or reproduced in any form.

26) D

27) B

28) C

29) unusual

30) D

31) B

32) "In my opinion daisies are the most beautiful flowers" or "Daisies are the most beautiful flowers in my opinion."

33) C

34) 2

35) B

36) D

37) inauspicious

38) B

39) C

40) A

41) B

42) 2

43) D

44) B

45) C

46) D

47) B

48) B

49) A

50) B

Wonderlic SLE Practice Test 2

1) A

2) unknown

3) B

4) C

5) D

6) B

7) C

8) C

9) D

10) B

11) D

12) D

13) D

14) C

15) A

16) C

17) C

18) C

19) B

20) D

21) A

22) B

23) "His favorite hobbies include swimming and reading" or "His favorite hobbies include reading and swimming."

24) D

25) 2

26) B

27) vehicle

28) C

29) B

30) D

31) C

32) D

33) He has a black belt in karate.

34) B

35) C

36) B

37) 2

38) C

39) B

40) B

41) C

42) B

43) C

44) D

45) fork

46) B

47) C

48) C

49) D

50) C

Wonderlic SLE Practice Test 3

1) B

2) B

3) C

4) C

5) D

6) D

7) The harder you work the more likely you are to succeed.

8) C

9) D

10) B

11) D

12) C

13) B

14) D

15) C

16) hardship

17) B

18) A

19) C

20) A

21) B

22) justify

23) B

24) "She is really a very kind person" or "She really is a very kind person."

25) D

26) D
27) C
28) C
29) 1
30) C
31) A
32) D
33) D
34) D
35) cleaning
36) B
37) A
38) C
39) D
40) C
41) D
42) C
43) D
44) C
45) D
46) C
47) C
48) A
49) C
50) 2

Wonderlic SLE Practice Test 4

1) C

2) D

3) C

4) D

5) A

6) D

7) 3

8) B

9) C

10) C

11) There are more business students this year than ever before.

12) A

13) students

14) A

15) C

16) D

17) B

18) D

19) A

20) B

21) C

22) A

23) C

24) C

25) C

26) D

27) 2

28) C

29) Eating ice cream too quickly can give you a headache.

30) B

31) prepare

32) C

33) A

34) A

35) B

36) D

37) D

38) C

39) C

40) D

41) A

42) A

43) D

44) accept

45) C

46) D

47) B

48) D

49) A

50) B

ANSWERS AND EXPLANATIONS

Wonderlic SLE Practice Test 1

1) The correct answer is B. Line up the numbers by the commas, and remember to carry the 1's:

$$\begin{array}{r} {\scriptstyle 1\ 1\ 1} \\ 1,594 \\ +23,786 \\ \hline 25,380 \end{array}$$

2) The correct answer is A. The woman is playing golf. Since everyone playing golf wears a blue shirt, according to the second statement, then the woman must be wearing a blue shirt.

3) The correct answer is A. Multiply 25 times $15 to get the answer: 25 × $15 = $375

4) The correct answer is 3. The pairs in the second, fourth, and fifth rows are duplicates.

5) The correct answer is A. For problems with decimals, line the figures up in a column and add zeros to fill in the column as shown below:

0.3500

0.0350

0.0530

0.3035

If you still struggle with decimals, you can remove the decimal points and the zeros before the other integers in order to see the answer more clearly.

~~0.3500~~

~~0.0350~~

~~0.0530~~

~~0.3035~~

When we have removed the zeros in front of the other numbers, we can clearly see that the largest number is 0.35.

6) The correct answer is B. "That's a cock and bull story" means that the story is unbelievable. "That doesn't hold water" means that something cannot be true.

7) The correct answer is C. Each panel is 8 feet 6 inches long, and he needs 11 panels to cover the entire side of the field. So, we need to multiply 8 feet 6 inches by 11, and then simplify the result. Step 1: 8 feet × 11 = 88 feet; Step 2: 6 inches × 11 = 66 inches; Step 3: There are 12 inches in a foot, so we need to determine how many feet and inches there are in 66 inches: 66 inches ÷ 12 = 5 feet 6 inches; Step 4: Now add the two results together. 88 feet + 5 feet and 6 inches = 93 feet and 6 inches.

8) The correct answer is A. The word "conceal" means to hide something. The word "obscure" means to cover something up.

9) The correct answer is B. In our problem, if $s\%$ of the students have been absent, then $100\% - s\%$ have not been absent. In other words, since a percentage is any given number out of 100%, the percentage of students who have not been absent is: $(100\% - s\%)$. This equation is then multiplied by the total number of students (x) in order to determine the answer: $(100\% - s\%) \times x$

10) The correct answer is D. The car is used for driving, just as the oven is used for cooking.

11) The correct answer is A. Put in zeros and line up the decimal points when you compare the numbers.

    0.0007

  A) 0.0012

  B) 0.0006

  C) 0.0022

  D) 0.0220

    0.0021

Answer choice B is less than 0.0007, and answer choices C and D are greater than 0.0021. Answer choice A (0.0012) is between 0.0007 and 0.0021, so it is the correct answer.

12) The correct answer is: A rolling stone gathers no moss.

13) The correct answer is A.

Subtract the up-front costs first of all: $40,000 – $3,700 = $36,300.

Then divide this figure by $500 to see how many projects can be completed.

$36,300 ÷ 500 = 72.6

Since a fraction of a project cannot be undertaken, the greatest number of projects is 72.

14) The correct answer is: farmer. All of the words pertain to things on a farm, but the farmer is the only human being on the list.

15) The correct answer is D. To answer this type of question, remember these basic principles: (a) Positive numbers are greater than negative numbers; (b) When

two fractions have the same numerator, the fraction with the smaller number in the denominator is the larger fraction. Accordingly, 1 is greater than $1/5$; $1/5$ is greater than $1/7$, and $1/7$ is greater than $-1/3$.

16) The correct answer is C. The proverb "You can't make an omelet without breaking a few eggs" means that a few mistakes or mishaps will inevitably occur when you are trying to achieve something.

17) The correct answer is A. The problem tells us that the morning flight had 52 passengers more than the evening flight, and there were 540 passengers in total on the two flights that day. Step 1: First of all, we need to deduct the difference from the total: 540 – 52 = 488; In other words, there were 488 passengers on both flights combined, plus the 52 additional passengers on the morning flight. Step 2: Now divide this result by 2 to allocate a number of passengers to each flight: 488 ÷ 2 = 244 passengers on the evening flight. (Had the question asked you for the number of passengers on the morning flight, you would have had to add back the number of additional passengers to find the total number of passengers for the morning flight: 244 + 52 = 296 passengers on the morning flight)

18) The correct answer is C. From the facts given in the three statements, we know that Mark dislikes whomever John likes, but we do not know conversely whether Mark likes whomever John dislikes. Therefore, we cannot be sure whether Mark likes Daryl.

19) The correct answer is B. There is a difference of 4 between each number in the sequence.

20) The correct answer is B. The captain does his or her job on a ship, just as a chef does his or her job in a kitchen.

21) The correct answer is C. Divide and then round up: 82 people in total ÷ 15 people served per container = 5.467 containers. We need to round up to 6 since we cannot purchase a fractional part of a container.

22) The correct answer is B. The word "insuperable" means impossible or insurmountable.

23) The correct answer is D. The question is asking us about a time duration of 6 minutes, so we need to calculate how many seconds there are in 6 minutes: 6 minutes × 60 seconds per minute = 360 seconds in total. Then divide the total time by the amount of time needed to make one journey: 360 seconds ÷ 45 seconds per journey = 8 journeys. Finally, multiply the number of journeys by the inches per journey in order to get the total inches: 10.5 inches for 1 journey × 8 journeys = 84 inches in total

24) The correct answer is B. First, determine how many cheese and pepperoni pizzas were sold. Each triangle symbol represents 5 pizzas. Therefore, 15 cheese pizzas were sold: 3 symbols on the pictograph × 5 pizzas per symbol = 15 cheese pizzas. We also know that 10 pepperoni pizzas were sold: 2 symbols on the pictograph × 5 pizzas per symbol = 10 pepperoni pizzas. Then determine the value of these two types of pizzas based on the prices stated in the problem: (15 cheese pizzas × $10 each) + (10 pepperoni pizzas × $12 each) = $150 + $120 = $270. The remaining amount is allocable to the vegetable pizzas: Total sales of $310 − $270 = $40 worth of vegetable pizzas. Since each triangle represents 5 pizzas, 5 vegetable pizzas were sold. We calculate the price of the vegetable pizzas as follows: $40 worth of vegetable pizzas ÷ 5 vegetable pizzas sold = $8 per vegetable pizza

25) The correct answer is C. The word "terse" means brusque or abrupt.

26) The correct answer is D. This is a problem on determining the value that is missing from the calculation of a mean of a set of values. Remember that the mean is the same thing as the arithmetic average. In order to calculate the mean, you simply add up the values of all of the items in the set, and then divide by the number of items in the set. Set up your equation to calculate the average, using x for the age of the 5th sibling:

$(2 + 5 + 7 + 12 + x) \div 5 = 8$

$(2 + 5 + 7 + 12 + x) \div 5 \times 5 = 8 \times 5$

$(2 + 5 + 7 + 12 + x) = 40$

$26 + x = 40$

$26 - 26 + x = 40 - 26$

$x = 14$

27) The correct answer is B. "People who live in glass houses shouldn't throw stones" means that you should not criticize someone for something if you do the same thing yourself.

28) The correct answer is C. If $\frac{x}{24}$ is between 8 and 9, x will need to be between 192 and 216, since $\frac{192}{24} = 192 \div 24 = 8$ and $\frac{216}{24} = 216 \div 24 = 9$. 200 is the only number from the answer choices that is greater than 192 and less than 216.

29) The correct answer is: unusual. Very few English words of this length contain three U's, so hopefully you were able to see the answer quickly.

30) The correct answer is D. We have the following numbers in our problem:

0.0012
0.0253
0.2135
0.3152

If you still do not feel confident with decimals, remember that you can remove the decimal point and the zeros after the decimal but before the other integers in order to see the answer more clearly.

12
253
2135
3152

31) The correct answer is B. "Amplify" means magnify or enlarge, so it is the opposite of diminish.

32) The correct answers are: "In my opinion daisies are the most beautiful flowers" or "Daisies are the most beautiful flowers in my opinion."

33) The correct answer is C. Work backwards based on the facts given. There are 18 students remaining at the end after one-fourth of them left for the principal's office. So, set up an equation for this:

$18 + \frac{1}{4}T = T$

$18 + \frac{1}{4}T - \frac{1}{4}T = T - \frac{1}{4}T$

$18 = \frac{3}{4}T$

$18 \times 4 = \frac{3}{4}T \times 4$

$72 = 3T$

$72 \div 3 = 3T \div 3$

$24 = T$

So, before the group of pupils left to see the principal, there were 24 students in the class. We know that one-fifth of the students left at the beginning to go to singing lessons, so we need to set up an equation for this.

$24 + \frac{1}{5}T = T$

$24 + \frac{1}{5}T - \frac{1}{5}T = T - \frac{1}{5}T$

$24 = \frac{4}{5}T$

$24 \times 5 = \frac{4}{5}T \times 5$

$120 = 4T$

$120 \div 4 = 4T \div 4$

$30 = T$

34) The correct answer is 2. The pairs in the first and fourth rows are exact duplicates. Be mindful of the punctuation in questions like this one.

35) The correct answer is B. At the beginning of January, there are 100 students, but 15% of the students leave during the month, so we have 85% left at the end of the month: 100 × 85% = 85. Then 15 students join on the last day of the month, so we add that back in to get to the total at the end of January: 85 + 15 = 100. If this pattern continues, there will always be 100 students in the class at the end of any month.

36) The correct answer is D. Calculate the discount: $120 × 12.5% = $15 discount. Then subtract the discount from the original price to determine the sales price: $120 – $15 = $105

37) The correct answer is: inauspicious. All of the other words in the set have positive connotations. "Inauspicious" means unfavorable or ill-boding.

38) The correct answer is B. Thus far, every other figure in the sequence is a square, so we need to have a square again to continue the sequence.

39) The correct answer is C. Divide by the fractional hour in order to determine the speed for an entire hour: 38.4 miles ÷ $4/5$ of an hour = 38.4 × $5/4$ = (38 × 5) ÷ 4 = 47.5 mph. We round this up to 48 mph.

40) The correct answer is A. The ratio of defective chips to functioning chips is 1 to 20. So, the defective chips form one group and the functioning chips form another group. Therefore, the total data set can be divided into groups of 21. Accordingly, $1/21$ of the chips will be defective. The factory produced 11,235 chips last week, so we calculate as follows: 11,235 × $1/21$ = 535

41) The correct answer is B. Subtract $2,550 from the total funds available of $55,000: $55,000 − $2,550 = $52,450. Then divide by $750 to determine how many residents can be accommodated $52,450 ÷ $750 = 69.9

It is not possible to accommodate a fractional part of one person, so we need to round down to 69 residents.

42) The correct answer is 2. The tenth month of the year is October. Don't let the numbers in front of the names of the months confuse you.

43) The correct answer is D. For problems that ask you to find the largest possible product of two even integers, first you need to divide the sum by 2. The sum in this problem is 30, so divide by 2: 30 ÷ 2 = 15. Now take the result from this division and find the 2 nearest even integers that are 1 number higher and lower: 15 + 1 = 16; 15 − 1 = 14. Finally, multiply these two numbers together in order to get the product: 16 × 14 = 224.

44) The correct answer is B. The word "implicate" means to blame or to incriminate, while the word "exonerate" means to set free from blame. So, the words have contradictory meanings.

45) The correct answer is C. Determine the dollar amount of the reduction or discount: $60 original price − $45 sale price = $15 discount. Then divide the discount by the original price to get the percentage of the discount: $15 ÷ $60 = 0.25 = 25%

46) The correct answer is D. Too many germs can lead to contamination, just as too much debt can lead to bankruptcy.

47) The correct answer is B. The sales price of each item is five times the cost. The cost is expressed as B, so the sales price is 5B. The difference between the sales price of item and the cost of each item is the profit: Sales Price − Cost = Profit. So, our expression is: 5B − B = 4B

48) The correct answer is B. The word "inchoate" means shapeless or undeveloped, so it is the opposite of developed.

49) The correct answer is A. By folding corner A to corner D, the sides of the cube are formed. Folding corner G to corner D forms the bottom of the cube, and corner E to corner H forms the top of the cube.

50) The correct answer is B. The words "extortionate" and "exorbitant" mean excessively expensive or unreasonable.

ANSWERS AND EXPLANATIONS

Wonderlic SLE Practice Test 2

1) The correct answer is A. Line up the decimal points as shown when adding. Always remember to carry the 1's.

    $$\begin{array}{r} {}^{11}\\ 4.25\\ 0.003\\ \underline{0.148}\\ 4.401 \end{array}$$

2) The correct answer is: unknown. For questions like this one, look for letters in multiples, such as the n's in this question, to help you solve the problem.

3) The correct answer is B. $7x$ is between 5 and 6, so set up an inequality as follows: $5 < 7x < 6$

    Then insert the fractions from the answer choices for the value of x to solve the problem.

    $5 < (7 \times {}^3/_4) < 6$

    $5 < [(7 \times 3) \div 4] < 6$

    $5 < (21 \div 4) < 6$

    $5 < 5.25 < 6$

    5.25 is between 5 and 6, so ³/₄ is the correct answer.

4) The correct answer is C. The proverb "Keep your friends close and your enemies closer" means that it is in your best interests to keep an eye on the actions of those who may be against you.

5) The correct answer is D. First of all, you need to determine the difference in temperature during the entire time period: 62 – 38 = 24 degrees less. Then

calculate how much time has passed. From 5:00 PM to 11:00 PM, 6 hours have passed. Next, divide the temperature difference by the amount of time that has passed to get the temperature change per hour: 24 degrees ÷ 6 hours = 4 degrees less per hour. To calculate the temperature at the stated time, you need to calculate the time difference. From 5:00 PM to 9:00 PM, 4 hours have passed. So, the temperature difference during the stated time is 4 hours × 4 degrees per hour = 16 degrees less. Finally, deduct this from the beginning temperature to get your final answer: 62°F − 16°F = 46°F.

6) The correct answer is B. The word "superlative" means top-notch or excellent, so it is the opposite of inferior.

7) The correct answer is C. For your first step, determine how many square feet there are in total: 2000 square feet per room × 8 rooms = 16,000 square feet in total. Then you need to divide by the coverage rate: 16,000 square feet to cover ÷ 900 square feet coverage per bucket = 17.77 buckets needed. It is not possible to purchase a partial bucket of paint, so 17.77 is rounded up to 18 buckets of paint.

8) The correct answer is C. The word "culminate" means to conclude or to come to an end.

9) The correct answer is D. Divide the distance traveled by the time in order to get the speed in miles per hour. Remember that in order to divide by a fraction, you need to invert the fraction, and then multiply.

$3.6 \text{ miles} \div 3/4 = 3.6 \times 4/3 = (3.6 \times 4) \div 3 = 14.4 \div 3 = 4.8 \text{ miles per hour}$

10) The correct answer is B. For your first step, add the subsets of the ratio together: 6 + 7 = 13. Then divide this into the total: 117 ÷ 13 = 9. Finally,

multiply the result from the previous step by the subset of males from the ratio: 6 × 9 = 54 males in the class.

11) The correct answer is D. The expression "A picture is worth a thousand words" means that you can understand a situation better visually by looking at a picture, rather than by reading a written description of the situation.

12) The correct answer is D. Remember that the mean is the same thing as the average. To find the average or the mean, add up all of the items in the set and then divide by the number of items in the set. Here we have 7 numbers in the set, so we get our answer as follows: (89 + 65 + 75 + 68 + 82 + 74 + 86) ÷ 7 = 539 ÷ 7 = 77

13) The correct answer is D. The area of a rectangle is equal to its length times its width. The field is 32 yards wide and 100 yards long, so now we can substitute the values.
Rectangle area = width × length
rectangle area = 32 × 100
rectangle area = 3200

14) The correct answer is C. Remember that the sum of all three angles within any triangle is always equal to 180 degrees. Deduct the degrees provided for angle A from 180° to find out the total degrees of the two other angles: 180° − 32° = 148°. Since this is an isosceles triangle, the remaining two angles have the same measurement. So, we need to divide by two in order to find out how many degrees each of the other angles has: 148° ÷ 2 = 74°

15) The correct answer is A. From the facts stated, we will know who the members are by looking at the signatures in the register. Signing the register is compulsory, so if someone has not signed it, then he or she is not a member.

16) The correct answer is C. Write out the formula: (length × 2) + (width × 2). Then substitute the values.

(17 × 2) + (4 × 2) = 34 + 8 = 42

17) The correct answer is C. The word "magnanimous" means charitable or altruistic, so it is the opposite of selfish or uncharitable.

18) The correct answer is C. The chart shows how many patients have survived. So, first of all you need to find the percentage for the patients that have not survived: 100% - 48% = 52%. Then multiply that percentage by the total for this category: 231,000 × 52% = 120,120

19) The correct answer is B. The word "sublime" means glorious or splendid, so it is similar in meaning to the word "superb."

20) The correct answer is D. The ratio of bags of carrots to bags of potatoes is 1 to 4, so for every bags of carrots, there are four bags of potatoes. So, take the total number of bags of carrots and multiply this by 4 to determine how many bags of potatoes there are in the store: 44 × 4 = 176.

21) The correct answer is A. The adjective "ingenious" can be used to describe an idea, just as the adjective "uneducated" can be used to describe ignorance.

22) The correct answer is B. Assign a variable for the age of the brothers as follows: Greg = G and William = W. Greg is three years older than twice the age of William. So, G = 3 + 2W. If Greg is 10 years old, then William is 23, because mathematically G = 3 + 2W = 3 + (2 × 10) = 23.

23) The correct answers are: "His favorite hobbies include swimming and reading" or "His favorite hobbies include reading and swimming."

24) The correct answer is D. 30 percent in decimal form equals to 0.30. The phrase "of what number" shows that we have to divide: 90 ÷ 0.30 = 300. We can check this result as follows: 300 × 0.30 = 90.

25) The correct answer is 2. Carefully compare the numbers, letters, and symbols in each item to those in the other item in each pair. Doing so, we can see that there are exact duplicates in rows 1 and 4.

26) The correct answer is B. To find the total amount contributed, you need to multiply: 31 × 12 = 372

27) The correct answer is: vehicle. All of the other words in the set describe places a vehicle could be taken, rather than a vehicle itself.

28) The correct answer is C. Remember that to represent a fraction as a decimal, you need to divide. So, you will need to do long division to determine the answer.

```
      .10
50)5.00
    5.00
       0
```

29) The correct answer is B. In twelve months, it will be January again, so we need to go six months after that to make up the 18 months. If we are in January of the next year and then add 6 months, we get July.

30) The correct answer is D. We know that Mary has already gotten 80% of the money. However, the question is asking how much money she still needs: 100% − 80% = 20% = 0.20. Now do the multiplication: $650 × 0.20 = $130

31) The correct answer is C. The word "genial" means cheerful or affable, while the word "adroit" means skillful. While both words have positive connotations, they are unrelated in meaning.

32) The correct answer is D. The question tells you the percentage of games the team lost, not won. Step 1: First of all, we have to calculate the percentage of games won. If the team lost 20 percent of the games, we know that the team won the remaining 80 percent.

    Step 2: Now do the long multiplication.

       50 games in total

    × .80 percentage of games won (in decimal form)

      40.0 total games won

33) The correct answer is: He has a black belt in karate. You should look for the word to place at the start of the sentence first and then try to match the adjectives with the remaining nouns.

34) The correct answer is B. Step 1: Look to see what information is common to both the question and to the information provided. Here we have the information that he can run 3 miles in 25 minutes. The question is asking how long it will take him to run 12 miles, so the commonality is miles. Step 2: Next, determine how many 3-mile increments there are in 12 miles: 12 ÷ 3 = 4. Step 3: Then you need to determine the time required to travel the stated distance. Accordingly, we need to multiply the time for 3 miles by 4: 25 minutes × 4 = 100. So, 100 minutes are needed to run 12 miles. Step 4: Finally, simplify into hours and minutes based on the fact that there are 60 minutes in one hour: 100 minutes = 1 hour 40 minutes.

35) The correct answer is C. Money can be placed into a bank, just as a foot can be placed into a shoe.

36) The correct answer is B. You can simplify the first fraction because both the numerator and denominator are divisible by 3: $^9/_6 \div {}^3/_3 = {}^3/_2$. Then divide the denominator of the second fraction by the denominator 2 of the simplified fraction $^3/_2$: $10 \div 2 = 5$. Now, multiply this number by the numerator of the first fraction to get your result: $5 \times 3 = 15$. You can check your answer as follows:

$^9/_6 = {}^{15}/_{10}$

$^9/_6 \div {}^3/_3 = {}^3/_2$

$^{15}/_{10} \div {}^5/_5 = {}^3/_2$

37) The correct answer is 2. There are exact duplicates in rows 2 and 3.

38) The correct answer is C. Remember that for questions like this one, you have to find the commonality between the facts in the question and the requested information for the solution. In this question, the commonality is the number of students. The question tells us that 17 out of every 20 students participate in a sport and that there are 800 total students. Step 1: Determine how many groups of 20 can be formed from the total of 800: $800 \div 20 = 40$ groups of 20 students in the school. Step 2: To solve the problem, you then need to multiply the number of participants per group by the possible number of groups. In this problem, there are 17 participants per every group of 20. There are 40 groups of 20. So, we multiply 17 by 40 to get our answer: $17 \times 40 = 680$ students.

39) The correct answer is B. The word "colossal" means huge or enormous, while the word "miniscule" means extremely small or tiny. So, the words have contradictory meanings.

40) The correct answer is B. We don't know the age of the 10th car, so set up an equation and put in the age of the 10th car as x to solve:

$(2 + 3 + 4 + 5 + 6 + 7 + 9 + 10 + 12 + x) \div 10 = 6$

$[(2 + 3 + 4 + 5 + 6 + 7 + 9 + 10 + 12 + x) \div 10] \times 10 = 6 \times 10$

$2 + 3 + 4 + 5 + 6 + 7 + 9 + 10 + 12 + x = 60$

$58 + x = 60$

$x = 2$

41) The correct answer is C. People who wear eyeglasses are intelligent according to statement 1, but that does not suggest that all intelligent people must wear eyeglasses.

42) The correct answer is B. The scores were: 9.9, 9.9, 8.2, 7.6 and 6.8. First, add them up: 6.8 + 7.6 + 8.2 + 9.9 + 9.9 = 42.4. Then divide the total by 5 to get the average since there are 5 scores: 42.4 ÷ 5 = 8.48

43) The correct answer is C. The expression "Fight fire with fire" means that you need to have a reaction that is as strong as the action that originally affected you. The expression "An eye for an eye, a tooth for a tooth" applies specifically to giving out a strong, serious punishment for a serious crime.

44) The correct answer is D. The volume of a box is calculated by taking the length times the width times the height: 5 × 6 × 10 = 300

45) The correct answer is: fork. All of the items in the list can be placed in the mouth, but the fork is the only item in the list that is not edible.

46) The correct answer is B. Calculate the total amount the family spent on main dishes: $8 × 4 = $32. Then deduct this from the total: $48 − $32 = $16. Finally, divide by 4 people to solve: $16 ÷ 4 = $4 per dessert.

47) The correct answer is C. The word "pernicious" means damaging, harmful, or dangerous.

48) The correct answer is C. Since there are 60 seconds in a minute, and heartbeats are measured in 10 second units, we divide the seconds as follows: 60 ÷ 10 = 6. Accordingly, the BPM is calculated by talking B times 6: BPM = B6.

49) The correct answer is D. In order to find the excess amount, we deduct the ideal BPM of 60 from the patient's actual BPM: BPM − 60

50) The correct answer is C. Shrimp is a type of seafood, just as trout is a type of fish.

ANSWERS AND EXPLANATIONS

Wonderlic SLE Practice Test 3

1) The correct answer is B. Divide the capacity by the time in order to get the rate: 1200 gallons ÷ 75 minutes = 16 gallons per minute.

2) The correct answer is B. The word "reticent" means reluctant to speak and the word "garrulous" means talkative, so the words have contradictory meanings.

3) The correct answer is C. First, multiply the erroneous average by the erroneous number of tests to get the total points: 78 × 8 = 624. Then divide this total by the correct number of tests: 624 ÷ 10 = 62.4

4) The correct answer is C. Yesterday the train traveled $117^3/_4$ miles, and today it traveled $102^1/_6$ miles. To find the difference, we subtract these two amounts. Because the fraction on the first mixed number is greater than the fraction on the second mixed number, we can subtract the whole numbers and the fractions separately: $117^3/_4$ miles – $102^1/_6$ miles = ? Step 1: Subtract the whole numbers: 117 – 102 = 15 miles. Step 2: Perform the operation on the fractions by finding the lowest common denominator. $^3/_4$ miles – $^1/_6$ miles = ?
So, we express the fractions $^3/_4$ miles + $^1/_6$ miles in their LCD form: $^3/_4$ × $^3/_3$ = $^9/_{12}$ and $^1/_6$ × $^2/_2$ = $^2/_{12}$. Then subtract these two fractions: $^9/_{12}$ – $^2/_{12}$ = $^7/_{12}$.
Step 3: Combine the results from the two previous steps to solve the problem: $117^3/_4$ miles – $102^1/_6$ miles = $15^7/_{12}$ miles.

5) The correct answer is D. Skiing is done in the snow, just as swimming is done in the water.

6) The correct answer is D. Sam is driving at 70 miles per hour, and at 10:30 am he is 140 miles from Farnam. Step 1: We need to find out how far he will be from Farnam at 11:00 am, so we need to work out how far he will travel in 30

minutes. Step 2: If Sam is traveling at 70 miles an hour, then he travels 35 minutes in half an hour: 70 miles in one hour × $1/2$ hour = 35 miles. Step 3: If he was 140 miles from Farnam at 10:30 am, he will be 105 miles from Farnam at 11:00 am: 140 − 35 = 105 miles

7) The correct answer is: The harder you work the more likely you are to succeed.

8) The correct answer is C. The twelve students who failed the test represent one-third of the class. Since one-third of the students have failed, we can think of the class as being divided into three groups: Group 1: The 12 students who failed; Group 2: 12 students who would have passed; Group 3: 12 more students who would have passed. So, the class consists of 36 students in total. In other words, we need to multiply by three to find the total number of students: 12 × 3 = 36

9) The correct answer is D. The expression "Beauty is in the eye of the beholder" means that the notion of what is beautiful can vary from person to person.

10) The correct answer is B. The problem tells us that sales this week were $600 and sales last week were $525. Step 1: First, we need to find the difference in sales between the two weeks: $600 - $525 = $75 more in sales this week. Step 2: Since each book is sold for $5, we divide this figure into the total in order to find out how many books were sold: $75 more sales ÷ $5 per book = 15 more books sold this week.

11) The correct answer is D. A percentage can always be expressed as a number with two decimal places. For example, 15% = 0.15 and 20% = 0.20. In our problem, 16% = 0.16. So D is correct.

12) The correct answer is C. August is six months after February. In other words, February is the second month of the year and adding 6 months to 2, we get the eighth month, which is August.

13) The correct answer is B. Step 1: First of all, you need to calculate the amount of the discount: $18 original price × 40% = $18 × 0.40 = $7.20 discount. Step 2: Then deduct the amount of the discount from the original price to calculate the sales price of the item: $18 original price - $7.20 discount = $10.80 sales price.

14) The correct answer is D. A black triangle has been added to each side of the black square as we go around the square clockwise.

15) The correct answer is C. Step 1: Calculate the amount of the tax increase: $480 original tax amount × 0.075 = $36 proposed increase in tax. Step 2: Then add the increase to the original amount to get the amount of the tax after the proposed increase: $480 original tax + $36 increase in tax = $516 tax after increase

16) The correct answer is: hardship. The other words in the list express positive situations, while "hardship" describes a negative situation.

17) The correct answer is B. If there are 12 children and each one is supposed to receive 4 items, we can do the calculation as follows: 12 children × 4 items per child = 48 items required in total. Now subtract the amount she already has from the total needed in order to determine how many more she needs: 48 items required in total – 40 items available = 8 items still needed.

18) The correct answer is A. The expression "The squeaky wheel gets the grease" means that the person who complains will be likely to have his or her complaint resolved, but those who say nothing will get nothing.

19) The correct answer is C. First of all, you have to find out how many students were absent on Tuesday. To find the number of absent students, you have to multiply the total number of students in the class by the percentage of the absence for Tuesday: 20 students in total × 5% = 1 student absent on Tuesday. Now calculate the absences for Wednesday in the same way: 20 students in total × 20% = 4 students absent on Wednesday. The problem is asking you how many more students were absent on Wednesday than Tuesday, so you need to subtract the two figures that you have just calculated. 4 students absent on Wednesday – 1 student absent on Tuesday = 3 students. So, 3 more students were absent on Wednesday.

20) The correct answer is A. The words "catalyst" and "impetus" both describe the cause of something.

21) The correct answer is B. The problem is asking you for the amount that the number of births per hospital in Johnson County for 2020 exceeded those for 1998. Step 1: First we have to calculate the amount for 2020. In order to calculate this figure, you have to divide the total births by the number of hospitals in each data set. For 2020, we have 240 total births and 15 hospitals in the data set: 240 ÷ 15 = 16 births per hospital for 2020. Step 2: Now calculate the amount for 1998. In our problem, this amount is provided. We can see that there were 12 births per hospital in Johnson County in 1998. Step 3: Now subtract the amounts for the two years to get your answer: 16 – 12 = 4 more births per hospital in 2020.

22) The correct answer is: justify. Another tip for questions like this one is to try to find word suffixes like -ify, -tion, or -ness.

23) The correct answer is B. The measurement of a straight line is 180° so the measurement of angle A is 180° − 109° = 71°. Since this is an isosceles triangle, angle A and angle B are equal. The sum of the degrees of the three angles of any triangle is 180°, so we subtract to find the measurement of angle A to solve: 180° − 71° − 71° = 38°.

24) The correct answers are: "She is really a very kind person" or "She really is a very kind person."

25) The correct answer is D. Step 1: You need to multiply the number of miles that she is going to travel by the amount of time it takes her to travel one mile: 17 minutes for 1 mile × 5 miles to travel = 85 minutes needed. Step 2: Now express the result in hours and minutes: 85 minutes − 60 minutes = 25 minutes. So, the answer is 1 hour and 25 minutes.

26) The correct answer is D. The problem tells us that Bart rides at a rate of 12 miles per hour. We know that he arrives in the town of Wilmington at 3:00 pm. The question is asking us how far Bart will be from Mount Pleasant at 5:00 pm. Step 1: Calculate the time difference: 5:00 pm − 3:00 pm = 2 hours difference. Step 2: Calculate the distance traveled: 12 miles per hour × 2 hours = 24 miles traveled. Step 3: Calculate the distance left. The town of Mount Pleasant is 50 miles from Wilmington: 50 miles to travel − 24 miles traveled = 26 miles left.

27) The correct answer is C. Milk can be used to make cheese, just as fabric can be used to make clothing.

28) The correct answer is C. The ticket office sold 360 more tickets on Friday than it did on Saturday. The office sold 2570 tickets in total during Friday and Saturday. Step 1: Subtract the excess: 2570 − 360 = 2210. Step 2: Allocate

the above figure to each day: 2210 ÷ 2 = 1105. Step 3: Calculate Friday's amount by adding back in the excess: 1105 + 360 = 1465.

29) The correct answer is 1. The pair in row 5 is an exact duplicate.

30) The correct answer is C. Step 1: Calculate the beginning height in inches. Remember that there are 12 inches in a foot: 5 feet × 12 inches per foot = 60 inches in height. Step 2: Calculate the increase in height: 60 inches × 10% = 6 inches. Step 3: Calculate the new height by adding the increase to the number at the beginning: 5 feet + 6 inches = 5 feet 6 inches.

31) The correct answer is A. The dog has just eaten chocolate, which we know makes dogs ill. So, the dog will become ill.

32) The correct answer is D. We know that we have to round to the nearest hundredth. The hundredth decimal place is the number 2 positions to the right of the decimal. For example, .01 is 1 one hundredth. In our question, the first jump of 3.246 is rounded up to 3.25. The second jump of 3.331 is rounded down to 3.33. The third jump of 3.328 is rounded up to 3.33. Then add these three figures together to get your answer: 3.25 + 3.33 + 3.33 = 9.91

33) The correct answer is D. The word "beleaguer" means to irritate or annoy, so it is the opposite of placate, which means appease.

34) The correct answer is D. You have to find the relationship between the number given in each row in the left column and the corresponding number in the right column. "9:50 am to 10:36 am" represents a journey time of 46 minutes. 11:15 to 12:01 is also 46 minutes, and so on. If we go 46 minutes back from 5:51 pm, we get 5:05 pm for our answer.

35) The correct answer is: cleaning. All of the other activities are things that are done for fun, while cleaning is usually considered to be a chore.

36) The correct answer is B. He owns 26 yachts and needs 6 feet 10 inches of rope for each one. Convert the feet and inches measurement to inches: 6 feet 10 inches = (6 × 12) + 10 inches = 72 + 10 = 82 inches. Then multiply by the number of items: 26 × 82 = 2132 inches of rope needed. Then convert back to feet and inches: 2132 inches ÷ 12 = 177 feet 8 inches.

37) The correct answer is A. The word "inculcate" means to indoctrinate or brainwash.

38) The correct answer is C. Step 1: You can simplify the first fraction because both the numerator and denominator are divisible by 3: $3/6 \div 3/3 = 1/2$. Step 2: Then divide the denominator of the second fraction ($^x/_{14}$) by the denominator of the simplified fraction ($1/2$) from above: 14 ÷ 2 = 7. Step 3: Now, multiply the number from step 2 by the numerator of the fraction we calculated in step 1 in order to get your result: 1 × 7 = 7. You can check your answer as follows:

$3/6 = 7/14$

$3/6 \div 3/3 = 1/2$

$7/14 \div 7/7 = 1/2$

39) The correct answer is D. Disappointment occurs when expectations are thwarted, just as desperation can occur when hope is thwarted.

40) The correct answer is C. There are 2 stars for speeding, and each star equals 30 violations, so there were 60 speeding violations in total. The fine for speeding is $50 per violation, so the total amount collected for speeding violations was: 60 speeding violations × $50 per violation = $3000. There are three stars for other violations, which is equal to 90 violations (3 × 30 = 90). Other violations are $20 each, so the total for other violations is: 90 × $20 = $1800. Next, we need to deduct these two amounts from the total collections of

$6,000 to find the amount collected for parking violations: $6000 − $3000 − $1800 = $1200 in total for parking violations. There is one star for parking violations, so there were 30 parking violations. We divide to get the answer: $1200 income for parking violations ÷ 30 parking violations = $40 each

41) The correct answer is D. The proverb "A bird in the hand is worth two in the bush" means that holding on to one certain opportunity is better than trying to pursue other uncertain opportunities. The proverb "Half a loaf is better than none" means that it is better to accept what one already has than to end up with nothing at all.

42) The correct answer is C. If she uses 12 cups of sugar, she is using 6 times the basic amount of 2 cups. (2 cups × 6 = 12 cups). So, to keep things in proportion, we also need to multiply the basic amount of one-third cup of butter by six: $1/3 × 6 = 2$ cups of butter

43) The correct answer is D. The word "abscond" means to disappear or escape, especially to avoid capture or legal punishment.

44) The correct answer is C. We know that she traveled 150 miles before the repair. Miles traveled before needing the repair: 60 MPH × 2.5 hours = 150 miles traveled. If the journey is 240 miles in total, she has 90 miles remaining after the car is repaired: 240 − 150 = 90. If she then travels at 75 miles an hour for 90 miles, the time she spends is: 90 ÷ 75 = 1.2 hours. There are 60 minutes in an hour, so 1.2 hours is 1 hour and 12 minutes because 60 minutes × 0.20 = 12 minutes. The time spent traveling after the repair is 1 hour and 12 minutes. Now add together all of the times to get your answer: Time spent before needing the repair: 2.5 hours = 2 hours and 30 minutes; Time spent waiting for the repair: 2 hours; The time spent traveling after the repair: 1 hour and 12 minutes; Total

time: 5 hours and 42 minutes. If she left home at 6:00 am, she will arrive in Denver at 11:42 am.

45) The correct answer is D. The word "redundant" means superfluous or unnecessary, so it is the opposite of necessary.

46) The correct answer is C. If the amount earned from selling jackets was one-third that of selling jeans, the ratio of jacket to jean sales was 1 to 3. So, we need to divide the total sales of $4,000 into $1,000 for jackets and $3,000 for jeans. We can then solve as follows: $3,000 in jeans sales ÷ $20 per pair = 150 pairs sold

47) The correct answer is C. According to the facts, sufferers of malaria have a fever, but not everyone with a fever has malaria.

48) The correct answer is A. The tank has a 500-gallon capacity and it is being filled at a rate of 3.5 gallons per minute, so we divide to get the time: 500 ÷ 3.5 = 142.85 minutes ≈ 2 hours and 23 minutes.

49) The correct answer is C. Digging is the purpose of the shovel, just as cutting is the purpose of a pair of scissors.

50) The correct answer is 2. There are exact duplicates in rows 3 and 5.

ANSWERS AND EXPLANATIONS

Wonderlic SLE Practice Test 4

1) The correct answer is C. Scholarly and academic are synonyms, just as intelligent and clever are synonyms.

2) The correct answer is D. The question provides the sequence: 2, 4, 8, 16. Try to find the pattern of relationship between the numbers. Here, we can see that:

   $2 \times 2 = 4$

   $4 \times 2 = 8$

   $8 \times 2 = 16$

   In other words, the next number in the sequence is always double the previous number. Therefore, the answer is: $16 \times 2 = 32$

3) The correct answer is C. Eating whole-grain products is good for you, but whole-grain products aren't the only ones that are good for you. So, the bread could be made from other wholesome ingredients.

4) The correct answer is D. Step 1: Convert into minutes the amount of time required to make one cap: 4 hours and 10 minutes = $(4 \times 60) + 10 = 240 + 10 = 250$ minutes needed to make one cap. Step 2: Multiply by the total output: 250 minutes × 12 caps = 3000 minutes. Step 3: Convert the total amount of minutes back to hours and minutes: 3000 minutes ÷ 60 = 50 hours.

5) The correct answer is A. The words "proclivity" and "predilection" both mean tendency, inclination, or preference, so the two words are synonyms.

6) The correct answer is D. Add the feet above ground to the feet below ground to get the total distance: 525 + 95 = 620 feet.

7) The correct answer is 3. The pairs in the first three rows are duplicates.

8) The correct answer is B. Step 1: Determine the value of the discount by multiplying the normal price by the percentage discount: $90 × 15% = $13.50 discount. Step 2: Subtract the value of the discount from the normal price to get the new price: $90 – $13.50 = $76.50.

9) The correct answer is C. The word "winsome" means attractive or appealing.

10) The correct answer is C. Step 1: You can express the fractions as decimals for the sake of simplicity: 10½ = 10.50; 7¾ = 7.75. Step 2: Then subtract to find the increase: 10.50 – 7.75 = 2.75. Step 3: Then convert back to a mixed number: 2.75 = 2¾

11) The correct answer is: There are more business students this year than ever before.

12) The correct answer is A. After her raise, she earns $184 per week. She continues to work 23 hours per week. Step 1: Determine the new hourly rate: $184 ÷ 23 hours = $8 per hour. Step 2: Determine the change in the hourly rate: $8 – $7.50 = 50 cents per hour.

13) The correct answer is: students. All of the people in the list can be found at a college or university, but the students are the only people in the list who do not work at the institution.

14) The correct answer is A. Step 1: Determine the distance traveled. If he is traveling 70 miles an hour, he will have traveled 70 miles after one hour has passed. Step 2: Determine the distance from the towns listed on the sign, considering that he has traveled for one hour. Washington: 140 – 70 = 70 miles from Washington; Yorkville: 105 – 70 = 35 miles from Yorkville; Zorster: 210 – 70 = 140 miles from Zorster. Step 3: Compare the above figures to your

answer choices to get your result. After an hour, he is 70 miles from Washington, so A is correct.

15) The correct answer is C. August is the eighth month of the year, so four months previous to the eighth month is the fourth month, which is April.

16) The correct answer is D. Step 1: Subtract the excess from the total: 300 − 114 = 186. Step 2: Allocate the difference into its respective parts. We are dividing the day into two parts: morning and afternoon. There were 186 cars in total without the excess, so divide this into two parts: 186 ÷ 2 = 93. Step 3: Determine the amount for the larger part. There were 114 more cars in the morning, so add this back in: 93 + 114 = 207 cars in the morning.

17) The correct answer is B. "Revile" and "reproach" both mean to blame or strongly disapprove of something.

18) The correct answer is D. A 12-pound container of item B costs $48. Therefore, it costs $4 per pound ($48 ÷ 12 pounds = $4 per pound). Item C costs 20% more per pound than item B. In other words, Item C costs 80 cents more ($4 × 20% = 0.80). So, the cost per pound of item C is $4.80.

19) The correct answer is A. Healing solves the problem of being wounded, just as mending solves the problem of being broken.

20) The correct answer is B. The cost of the photography course is $20 per week plus a $5 fee per week for review of photographs and administration. So, the course costs $25 per week. To get the total cost we need to multiply by the number of weeks, which is represented by variable W. Therefore, the total cost of the course and fees for W weeks is $25 × W = $25W.

21) The correct answer is C. The word "impeccable" means without fault, while the word "impecunious" means being penniless or in the state of poverty. So, the words have unrelated meanings.

22) The correct answer is A. Remember that when two fractions have the same numerator, the fraction with the smaller number in the denominator is the larger fraction. So, –¹/₄ is less than ¹/₈, ¹/₈ is less than ¹/₆, and ¹/₆ is less than 1.

23) The correct answer is C. She could work in a part of the court house that does not deal with civil procedures.

24) The correct answer is C. This question asks you to interpret a graph in order to determine the price per unit of an item. To solve the problem, look at the graph and then divide the total sales in dollars by the total quantity sold in order to get the price per unit. For ten hamburgers, the total price is $85, so each hamburger sells for $8.50: $85 total sales in dollars ÷ 10 hamburgers sold = $8.50 each. The cost of shakes is represented by: $c = \frac{9}{4}s = (9 \div 4)s = 2.25s$, so each shake costs $2.25. So, the difference between the cost of one hamburger and the cost of one shake is $8.50 – $2.25 = $6.25

25) The correct answer is C. The word "lassitude" means weariness or exhaustion.

26) The correct answer is D. The tenths place is the first place to the right of the decimal, so 12.86749 rounded to the nearest tenth is 12.9. We have to round up because the number in the hundredths place is 6, which is 5 or greater.

27) The correct answer is 2. There are exact duplicates in rows 3 and 5.

28) The correct answer is C. The distance between point B and point C is 1.2. Point B is at 0.35, so point C is either 0.35 – 1.2 = –0.85 or 0.35 + 1.2 = 1.55.

29) The correct answer is: Eating ice cream too quickly can give you a headache.

30) The correct answer is B. 15.845 + 8.21 = 24.055. Rounding to the nearest integer, we remove the decimals to get 24.

31) The correct answer is: prepare. All of the items in the list are verbs, but the word "prepare" is the only one that does not describe an injury to the body.

32) The correct answer is C. Three out of ten students are taking the class. So, here we have the proportion 3 to 10. Step 1: Divide the total number of students by the second number in the proportion to get the number of groups: 650 ÷ 10 = 65 groups. Step 2: Multiply the number of groups by the first number in the proportion in order to get the result: 3 × 65 = 195 art students.

33) The correct answer is A. A bird is part of a flock, just as a sheep is part of a herd.

34) The correct answer is A. Remember to put in zeros and line up the decimal points when you compare the numbers.

0.5400

0.0540

0.0450

0.5045

Therefore, the largest number is 0.540

35) The correct answer is B. The expression "Never look a gift horse in the mouth" means that you should not refuse or be unappreciative of gifts that are offered to you.

36) The correct answer is D. The first three bars of the graph represent the first 30 minutes, so add these three together for your answer: 1.5 + 1.2 + 0.8 = 3.5 miles

37) The correct answer is D. The word "accost" means to confront, so it is the opposite of the word "shun," which means to stay away from someone.

38) The correct answer is C. He is using 14 ounces of plaster powder, so divide that by the basic amount of plaster of 4 ounces, stated in the instructions. 14 ÷ 4 = 3.5. Then multiply this result by the basic amount of water of 3 ounces, stated in the instructions: 3 × 3.5 = 10.5

39) The correct answer is C. The word "console" means to support, comfort, or sympathize, so it is the opposite of antagonize.

40) The correct answer is D. Each number in the sequence is found by multiplying by 3.

2 × 3 = 6

6 × 3 = 18

18 × 3 = 54

54 × 3 = 162

41) The correct answer is A. "Dexterous" means adroit, skillful, or adept.

42) The correct answer is A. Subtract the two amounts and then do the rounding. 15,138 − 9,927 = 5,211 (Rounded to 5,000). Check by rounding the individual amounts as follows: 15,000 − 10,000 = 5,000

43) The correct answer is D. If it is 10% cooler today, today's temperature is 90% of yesterday's temperature. So, today's temperature is 90 degrees × 90% = 81 degrees

44) The correct answer is: accept. Having the letter c twice is unusual, so you should try to structure your answer around this.

45) The correct answer is C. This is essentially a mixed number problem. Here you can covert the fraction to decimals to make the subtraction easier.

15½ – 2¼ = 15.5 – 2.25 = 13.25 = 13¼

46) The correct answer is D. The four sides of the cube are formed by joining corners D and E. Corner H folds down to corner E to form the top of the cube, and corner A folds up to corner C to form the bottom of the cube.

47) The correct answer is B. Convert to a fraction with 100 in the denominator in order to find the percentage: $^2/_{10} = {}^{20}/_{100} = 20\%$

48) The correct answer is D. You can create an equation to set out the facts of this problem. Here we will say that the total number of students is variable S.

15 = (S – ¼S) × ½

15 = ¾S × ½

15 = $^3/_8$S

15 × 8 = $^3/_8$S × 8

120 = 3S

S = 40

49) The correct answer is A. The expression "There's no such thing as a free lunch" means that it is impossible to get something for nothing.

50) The correct answer is B. In order to calculate a discount, you must first determine how much the item was marked down.

$150 – $120 = $30

Then divide the mark down by the original price.

30 ÷ 150 = 0.20

Finally, convert the decimal to a percentage.

0.20 = 20%

APPENDIX 1 – 40 MATH WARM-UP EXERCISES

1) 7.23 + .004 + .513 = ?

2) 8.13 × 3.1 = ?

3) Two people are going to give money to a foundation for a project. Person A will provide one-half of the money. Person B will donate one-eighth of the money. What fraction represents the unfunded portion of the project?

4) Convert the following to decimal format: $3/20$

5) 60 is 20 percent of what number?

6) 6¾ – 2½ = ?

7) Estimate the result of the following: 12.9 × 3.1

8) Express 30 percent of y as a fraction with 100 as the denominator.

9) 152 ÷ 8 = ?

10) 7.55 + .055 + .02 = ?

11) Estimate the result of the following: 502 ÷ 4.9

12) Beth took a test that had 60 questions. She got 10% of her answers wrong. How many questions did she answer correctly?

13) 4.602 − 0.32 = ?

14) 4.27 × 3.1 = ?

15) A job is shared by 4 workers, A, B, C, and D. Worker A does 1/6 of the total hours. Worker B does 1/3 of the total hours. Worker C does 1/6 of the total hours. What fraction represents the remaining hours allocated to person D?

16) 120 students took a math test. The 60 female students in the class had an average score of 95, while the 60 male students in the class had an average of 90. What is the average test score for all 120 students in the class?

17) $3\frac{1}{2} - 2\frac{2}{5}$ = ?

18) 0.18 ÷ 0.06 = ?

19) $\frac{1}{32}$ is equivalent to what percentage?

20) 1/3 − 1/7 = ?

21) A class contains 20 students. On Tuesday 5% of the students were absent. On Wednesday 20% of the students were absent. How many more students were absent on Wednesday than on Tuesday?

22) Farmer Brown owns a herd of cattle. This year, his herd consisted of 250 cows. Then he sold 60% of his herd. How many cows did he sell?

23) Estimate the result of the following: $30^{1}/_{4} \times 8^{9}/_{10}$

24) $6.55 \times 1.1 = ?$

25) Three people are going to contribute money to a charity. Person A will provide one-third of the money. Person B will contribute one-half of the money. What fraction represents Person C's contribution of money for the project?

26) The snowfall for November is 5 inches more than for December. If the total snowfall for November and December is 35 inches, what was the snowfall for November?

27) $2/3 - 1/6 = ?$

28) A museum counts its visitors each day and rounds each daily figure up or down to the nearest 10 people. 104 people visit the museum on Monday, 86 people visit the museum on Tuesday, and 81 people visit the museum on Wednesday. What amount best represents the number of visitors to the museum for the three days, after rounding?

29) Convert the following fraction into decimal format: $4/50$

30) $5\frac{1}{3} - 1\frac{1}{4} = ?$

31) $1.25 + .655 + .002 = ?$

32) Shania is entering a talent competition which has three events. The third event (C) counts three times as much as the second event (B), and the second event counts twice as much as the first event (A). What equation, expressed only in terms of variable A, can be used to calculate Shania's final score for the competition?

33) $(-12 + 6) \div 3 = ?$

34) $-6(4 - 1) - 2(5 - 2) = ?$

35) $(3 + -13) \div 5 = ?$

36) $(-12 + 8) \div 2 = ?$

37) $-5(3 - 1) - 2(5 - 7) = ?$

38) $(-10 + 1) \div 3 = ?$

39) A car travels at 60 miles per hour. The car is currently 240 miles from Boston. How long will it take for the car to get to Boston?

40) The price of socks is $2 per pair and the price of shoes is $25 per pair. Anna went shopping for socks and shoes, and she paid $85 in total. In this purchase, she bought 3 pairs of shoes. How many pairs of socks did she buy?

APPENDIX 2 – SOLUTIONS TO THE MATH WARM-UP EXERCISES

1) The correct answer is: 7.747

   When you add on your scratch paper, be sure to line all of the decimals up in a column like this:

   7.230
   0.004
   0.513
   ─────
   7.747

   As you can see, you should add zeros where necessary at the beginning or end of the numbers in order to make the decimal points line up.

2) The correct answer is: 25.203

   Tip: Be sure to put the decimal point in the correct position after you do the long multiplication.

   We know that the decimal point has to be three places from the right on the final product because 8.13 has 2 decimal places and 3.1 has 1 decimal place, so 1 plus 2 equals 3 places.

   ```
       8.13
   ×    3.1
       ────
        .813
      24.390
      ──────
      25.203
   ```

3) The correct answer is: 3/8

   The sum of all contributions must be equal to 100%, simplified to 1. Let's say that the variable U represents the unfunded portion of the project. So the equation that represents this problem is: A + B + U = 1. Substitute with the fractions that have been provided: 1/2 + 1/8 + U = 1

   Then use the lowest common denominator for the fractions.

   4/8 + 1/8 + U = 1

   5/8 + U = 1

　　　　　U = 1 − 5/8

　　　　　U = 3/8

4)　　　The correct answer is: 0.15

　　　　In order to convert a fraction to a decimal, you must do long division until you have no remainder.

```
       .15
20)3.00
     2.0
     1.00
     1.00
        0
```

5)　　　The correct answer is: 300. 20 percent is equal to 0.20. The phrase "of what number" indicates that we need to divide the two amounts given in the problem: 60 ÷ 0.20 = 300. We can check this result as follows: 30 × 0.20 = 60

6)　　　The correct answer is: 4¼. Questions like this test your knowledge of mixed numbers. Mixed numbers are those that contain a whole number and a fraction. If the fraction on the first mixed number is greater than the fraction on the second mixed number, you can subtract the whole numbers and the fractions separately. Remember to use the lowest common denominator on the fractions.
6 − 2 = 4

3/4 − 1/2 = 3/4 − 2/4 = 1/4

Therefore, the result is 4¼.

7)　　　The correct answer is: 39. For estimation problems like this, round the decimals up or down to the nearest whole number. 12.9 is rounded up to 13, and 3.1 is rounded down to 3. Then do long multiplication.

```
     13
   ×  3
     39
```

8) The correct answer is: 30y/100. This question tests your knowledge of how to express percentages as fractions. Percentages can always be expressed as that number over one hundred. So 30% = 30/100.

9) The correct answer is: 19

You must do long division until you have no remainder.

```
        19
    8) 152
        8
        72
        72
         0
```

10) The correct answer is: 7.625. Remember to line up the decimal points when you add.

7.550
0.055
0.020
7.625

11) The correct answer is: 100. Remember to round the numbers up or down to the nearest whole number. 502 is rounded down to 500, and 4.9 is rounded up to 5. Then divide: 500 ÷ 5 = 100

12) The correct answer is: 54. You must first determine the percentage of questions that Beth answered correctly. We know that she got 10% of the answers wrong, so therefore the remaining 90% were correct.
Now we multiply the total number of questions by the percentage of correct answers: 60 × 90% = 54

13) The correct answer: 4.282. Subtract the numbers on your scratch paper, being sure to line the decimals up in a column.

 4.602
−0.320
 4.282

14) The correct answer is: 13.237

Be careful with the decimal point positions when you do long multiplication.

```
    4.27
×   3.1
    .427
 12.810
 13.237
```

15) The correct answer is: 1/3. The sum of the work from all four people must be equal to 100%, simplified to 1. In other words, they make up the total hours by working together.

A + B + C + D = 1

1/6 + 1/3 + 1/6 + D = 1

Now, find the lowest common denominator of the fractions.

3×2 is 6. So the lowest common denominator is 6.

Now convert the fractions as required.

$1/3 \times 2/2 = 2/6$

Now add the fractions together.

1/6 + 2/6 + 1/6 + D = 1

4/6 + D = 1

4/6 − 4/6 + D = 1 − 4/6

D = 1 − 4/6

D = 2/6 = 1/3

16) The correct answer is: 92.5. You need to find the total points for all the females and the total points for all the males. Then add these two amounts together and divide by the total number of students in the class to get your solution.

Females: 60 × 95 = 5700

Males: 60 × 90 = 5400

(5700 + 5400) ÷ 120 = 11,100 ÷ 120 = 92.5

17) The correct answer is: $1^1/_{10}$. Remember that if the fraction on the first mixed number is greater than the fraction on the second mixed number, you can subtract the whole numbers and the fractions separately.

   $3 - 2 = 1$

   $1/2 - 2/5 = 5/10 - 4/10 = 1/10$

   Therefore, the result is $1^1/_{10}$

18) The correct answer is: 3. You must do long division until you have no remainder. Remember to line up the decimal points.

   ```
         3.0
   .06) .18
        .18
          0
   ```

19) The correct answer is: 3.125%

   $1 \div 32 = 0.03125$

   $0.03125 = 3.125\%$

20) The correct answer is: 4/21. First, find the lowest common denominator.

   $1/3 \times 7/7 = 7/21$

   $1/7 \times 3/3 = 3/21$

   When you have got both fractions in the same denominator, you subtract them.

   $7/21 - 3/21 = 4/21$

21) The correct answer is: 3. Figure out the amount of absences for the two days and then subtract.

   Tuesday's absences: $20 \times 5\% = 1$

   Wednesday's absences: $20 \times 20\% = 4$

   $4 - 1 = 3$

22) The correct answer is: 150. Express the percentage as a decimal: $60\% = 0.60$

   Then multiply to solve: $250 \times .60 = 150$

23) The correct answer is: 270. Remember to round the fractions up or down to the nearest whole number. Then do the multiplication: 30 × 9 = 270

24) The correct answer is: 7.205

Remove the decimal points:
655 × 11 = (655 × 10) + (655 × 1) =
6550 + 655 = 7205
6.55 has a decimal point two places from the right. 1.1 has a decimal point 1 place from the right. So, we know that we have to put the decimal point *three* numbers from the right on the final product of 7205. Therefore, the final answer is 7.205

25) The correct answer is: 1/6. The three people make up the whole contribution by paying in together, so the sum of contributions from all three people must be equal to 100%, simplified to 1.

A + B + C = 1
1/3 + 1/2 + C = 1
Now, find the lowest common denominator of the fractions.
2/6 + 3/6 + C = 1
Therefore, C = 1/6

26) The correct answer is: 20 inches. Subtract the difference in snowfall between the two months from the total snowfall for the two months, and then divide by 2 in order to get the December snowfall.

35 − 5 = 30

30 ÷ 2 = 15

Now add back the excess for November to get the total for November.

15 + 5 = 20

27) The correct answer is: 1/2

First, find the lowest common denominator.

2/3 × 2/2 = 4/6

When you have got both fractions in the same denominator, you subtract them.

4/6 – 1/6 = 3/6, simplified to 1/2

28) The correct answer is: 270. Do the rounding for each day separately (before doing the addition) because this is stipulated in the problem. Then add together to solve the problem.

104 Rounded to 100

86 Rounded to 90

81 Rounded to 80

100 + 90 + 80 = 270

29) The correct answer is: 0.08

Do long division until you have no remainder.

```
      .08
50)4.00
    4.00
       0
```

Alternatively, you know that 50 goes into 100 two times. So you can avoid long division by multiplying the numerator by 2 and adding a decimal point: 4 × 2 = 8% = .08

30) The correct answer is: $4^{1}/_{12}$

Subtract the whole numbers and the fractions separately, and use the lowest common denominator on the fractions.

5 – 1 = 4

1/3 – 1/4 = 4/12 – 3/12 = 1/12

Therefore, the result is $4^{1}/_{12}$.

31) The correct answer is: 1.907

Remember to line up the decimal points as shown.

1.250
0.655
<u>0.002</u>
1.907

32) The correct answer is: 9A

Final Score = A + B + C

B = 2A

C = 3B = 3 × 2A = 6A

Now express the original equation in terms of A:

A + B + C = A + 2A + 6A = 9A

33) The correct answer is: −2

Deal with the part of the equation inside the parentheses first.

(−12 + 6) ÷ 3 =

−6 ÷ 3

Then do the division.

−6 ÷ 3 = −2

34) The correct answer is: −24

Complete the operations inside the parentheses first.

Remember to be careful when multiplying the negative numbers.

−6(4 − 1) − 2(5 − 2) =

−6(3) − 2(3) =

(−6 × 3) − (2 × 3) =

−18 − 6 =

−24

35) The correct answer is: −2

Deal with the part of the equation inside the parentheses first.

(3 + −13) ÷ 5 =

−10 ÷ 5

Then do the division.

−10 ÷ 5 = −2

36) The correct answer is: −2. Deal with the part of the equation inside the parentheses first: (−12 + 8) ÷ 2 = −4 ÷ 2

Then do the division: −4 ÷ 2 = −2

37) The correct answer is: −6

Remember to complete the operations inside the parentheses first and to be careful when multiplying the negative numbers.

−5(3 − 1) − 2(5 − 7) =

−5(2) − 2(−2) =

(−5 × 2) − (2 × −2) =

−10 + 4 = −6

38) The correct answer is: −3

Deal with the part of the equation inside the parentheses first.

(−10 + 1) ÷ 3 = −9 ÷ 3

Then do the division: −9 ÷ 3 = − 3

39) The correct answer is: 4 hours. Remember to read questions like this one very carefully. If the car travels at 60 miles an hour and needs to go 240 more miles, we need to divide the miles to travel by the miles per hour.

miles to travel ÷ miles per hour = time remaining

So, if we substitute the values from the question, we get:

240 ÷ 60 = 4

In other words, the remaining time is 4 hours.

40) The correct answer is: 5 pairs

Calculate the amount spent on shoes: $25 \times 3 = \$75$. Then subtract this from the total: $85 - \$75 = \$10$. Then divide by the cost of a pair of socks to solve: $10 \div \$2 = 5$ pairs of socks

www.ingramcontent.com/pod-product-compliance
Lightning Source LLC
Chambersburg PA
CBHW081750100526
44592CB00015B/2370